MCP AI Agents

A Practical Guide to Building Context-Aware Agents with Claude, OpenAI, and Beyond

Written By

Dr. Maxwell Brooks

This book is a work of technical reference. While every effort has been made to ensure the accuracy of the information contained herein, the author and publisher make no warranties, express or implied, with respect to the accuracy or completeness of the contents. The advice and strategies presented may not be suitable for your specific situations. Consult a qualified professional where appropriate.

For the latest updates, errata, and companion source code, visit the official repository. For permissions or bulk orders.

Table of Contents

Preface

A. Why This Book (Revised Edition)

The rapid evolution of large language models has transformed ambitious prototypes into mission-critical systems. Yet until now, bridging the gap between a conversational LLM and real-world applications has required cobbling together disparate tutorials, hacks, and half-baked code snippets. This revised edition of **MCP AI Agents** exists to change that. It delivers a unified, battle-tested methodology for building **context-aware agents**—applications that don't just chat, but act—using Claude, OpenAI, and any future LLM that supports the open Model Context Protocol (MCP).

From day one, you'll move beyond theory to working code. In Chapter 1, for instance, you'll load the official MCP specification, inspect the JSON-RPC tool manifest directly from the Anthropic GitHub, and spin up your first "hello, world" tool server in under five minutes. You'll see exactly how the manifest defines a `summarize_text` endpoint—complete with parameter schemas and error codes—and how Claude uses that schema to construct a valid tool call, invoke your server, and render the result back into the chat.

As you progress, each chapter doubles as a hands-on lab. When you reach the section on multi-tool orchestration, you won't merely read about LangGraph's architecture—you'll clone the official LangGraph example repo, extend its node definitions with a new `query_sql` tool drawn from the MCP spec, and observe how Claude routes context through your custom workflow. Later, you'll package that entire stack into Docker containers and deploy to Render with a single CLI command, mirroring the exact steps shown in the companion repository.

This book's promise—and its revision—is simple: every concept you learn is instantly runnable, verifiable, and extensible. By the end, you'll not only understand the why behind context-aware AI, you'll have a production-ready codebase and a robust, versioned GitHub repository that reflects the most current best practices. Whether you're automating business reports, orchestrating multi-agent teams, or building your first personal assistant, this revised edition gives you the tools, examples, and deployment paths to ship real-world, context-driven agents with confidence.

B. Who This Book Is For?

This book is written for AI developers, ML engineers, and system architects who have already built simple chatbots or experimented with language models but now need to integrate those models into real, production-grade systems. You're the person who, instead of asking "What can GPT-4 do?" asks "How do I connect GPT-4 to my database, file system, or custom APIs so it can act on real data?" If you've ever spent hours wrestling with half-baked code samples or struggled to get Claude—or any LLM—to reliably call your tool, this guide is precisely what you need.

Imagine you're following the Anthropic documentation to expose a `summarize_text` endpoint via MCP. In the official example, you clone the sample repo, inspect the `tool_manifest.json`, and see how `input_schema` enforces that `text` must be a string. You then write a FastAPI handler that reads that schema, validates incoming JSON-RPC calls from Claude, and returns a neatly structured summary. Within minutes, you've gone from reading theory to invoking a live tool—no more guessing how prompts and tool calls should line up. This book shows you exactly how to reproduce and extend that example for dozens of tools: search, database queries, PDF parsing, you name it.

By the end of this book, you'll have the skills to design, build, and deploy context-aware agents that do more than answer questions—they integrate, automate, and orchestrate in real-world environments. Whether your next project is a research assistant that cites sources, a business report generator that emails stakeholders, or a multi-agent workflow running on Kubernetes, you'll know precisely how to apply the MCP spec, secure your endpoints, and ship maintainable code. This book is for professionals who demand more than a chat interface—they want systems that think, decide, and act.

C. What You'll Learn

In this book, you'll learn how to transform language models from isolated chat engines into fully integrated agents that operate in real environments. You start by mastering the Model Context Protocol—loading the official MCP specification, examining the `tool_manifest.json` provided by Anthropic, and running through a live example where you define an `echo` tool, validate its JSON-RPC schema, and invoke it from Claude within minutes. This hands-on exercise shows you exactly how the manifest's `input_schema` and `output_schema` drive every request and response, eliminating guesswork from prompt engineering.

Next, you'll build increasingly sophisticated tools: a file reader that parses local Markdown or PDF using the official Claude tool examples; a web scraper that filters HTML by URL patterns as demonstrated in the Anthropic code samples; and an API wrapper that retrieves weather, news, or financial data before feeding it back into GPT-4 via OpenAI's function-calling interface. Each tool chapter walks you through cloning the companion repository, extending the provided server code, and testing it with real JSON-RPC calls in Postman or curl.

Armed with these primitives, you'll orchestrate multi-step workflows—chaining a database query to a summarizer, or combining search results and citation formatting in a research agent—using LangGraph state machines and CrewAI role-based pipelines drawn from the community examples. You'll see how to embed Claude's streaming outputs into your observability stack, catch malformed JSON in real time, and write unit tests that simulate prompt-to-tool flows.

Finally, you'll package your agent stack into Docker containers and deploy to Railway, Render, or Fly.io with a single CLI command, securing endpoints with bearer tokens and integrating CI/CD pipelines as shown in the official deployment templates. By the end of the book, you'll not only understand the theory of context-aware AI, you'll have a verifiable, production-ready codebase and live endpoints running in the cloud—ready to replace brittle prototypes with scalable, maintainable, real-world agents.

D. How This Book Is Organized

This book is laid out as a clear, progressive journey—from understanding the underlying protocol to shipping fully containerized, multi-agent systems in production. In **Part I**, we ground you in the fundamentals of context-aware AI and the Model Context Protocol. You'll begin by loading the official MCP specification from Anthropic's GitHub, inspecting the `tool_manifest.json`, and running your first JSON-RPC "hello, world" call against Claude. This foundation ensures you never build on sand.

Moving into **Part II**, we shift to hands-on tool development and environment setup. You'll clone the companion repository's starter project, install the MCP SDK and Claude/OpenAI clients, and spin up your first FastAPI-based tool server. Following the official FastAPI examples, you'll validate inputs, handle errors, and invoke your tool from Claude in real time. By the end of this section, you'll have a working "Hello, Tool World" server running locally and responding to genuine JSON-RPC calls.

In **Part III**, you'll build a library of practical tools—file readers, web scrapers, API wrappers—each chapter demonstrating how to extend official Anthropic code samples. For example, you'll adapt the provided PDF parser example to extract and summarize Markdown, then chain that output through OpenAI's function-calling endpoint to generate polished reports. This section teaches you how to compose and embed context, turning isolated utilities into cohesive workflows.

Parts IV and V deepen your skills with multi-tool agents and orchestration frameworks. Drawing on the LangGraph and CrewAI examples in the official documentation, you'll define state machines that route context through custom tools, handle failures, and coordinate multiple agents in parallel. You'll see exactly how to register these tools in MCP, trigger transitions, and resume workflows after interruptions—no more one-off scripts.

In **Part VI**, you apply everything in full-stack projects: a Claude research assistant, a business report generator, a support ticket bot, and a personal productivity planner. Each project begins with a real-world user story, walks through manifest definitions, code templates, and prompt engineering guidelines, and concludes with step-by-step deployment to Railway or Fly.io via the official CLI pipelines.

Finally, **Part VII** covers evaluation, security, and deployment best practices—streaming logs, schema validation, Dockerization, CI/CD, and regulatory compliance—while **Part VIII** explores the broader MCP ecosystem, community tooling, and future trends. **Part IX** houses appendices with quick references, blueprints, and CLI cheatsheets. Throughout, every concept is tethered directly to the official source examples and the live code repo, so you always know exactly where to find, run, and extend the material. By following this organization, you'll build both deep understanding and a production-ready codebase by the last page.

E. Companion Resources & Live Code Repo

Every chapter in this book is accompanied by fully runnable source code, configuration files, and deployment scripts hosted in the **Companion GitHub Repository**. Rather than hunting for fragments scattered across multiple repos, you'll find a single, versioned project that mirrors the book's organization—complete with PartI/, PartII/, ... PartIX/ directories. In each folder, you'll see the exact tool_manifest.json, Python or TypeScript server code, prompt templates, Dockerfiles, and test suites used in the text.

For example, in PartII/Chapter05, you'll open the hello_tool_server directory and run:

```
git clone https://github.com/your-org/mcp-ai-agents.git
cd mcp-ai-agents/PartII/Chapter05/hello_tool_server
pip install -r requirements.txt
uvicorn server:app --reload
```

These steps spin up the same FastAPI server you read about, with JSON-RPC endpoints defined in the official Anthropic example. A matching Postman collection and curl snippets live alongside, so you can invoke the summarize_text endpoint exactly as shown, inspect the real JSON-RPC traffic, and iterate on the code immediately.

Throughout the repo you'll also find:

- **Environment templates** (.env.example) for Claude and OpenAI API keys
- **CI workflows** under .github/workflows that automatically lint, test, and build Docker images on every pull request
- **Render, Railway, and Fly.io deployment manifests** so you can deploy in minutes, using the same render.yaml and fly.toml files referenced in Chapter 18
- **Issue templates** and a CONTRIBUTING.md guide that explain how to report errata, suggest enhancements, or contribute new tools to the MCP ecosystem

By the time you finish the book, you'll not only understand the theory and patterns of context-aware AI, you'll also have a clean, battle-tested codebase you can fork, extend, and deploy in your own organization—guaranteeing that every example you study is instantly runnable, verifiable, and production-ready.

Part I | Foundations of MCP & Context-Aware AI

Chapter 1 | Introduction to Context-Aware Agents

1.1 What Is the Model Context Protocol (MCP)?

The Model Context Protocol, or MCP, is the open specification that turns a language model from a passive text generator into an active, context-aware agent. At its core, MCP defines a JSON-RPC 2.0 interface: a manifest file declares each tool's name, purpose, input schema, and output schema, and the agent—Claude, OpenAI, or any compatible model—uses that manifest to plan, invoke, and consume tool calls in a structured, unambiguous way.

When you load the official MCP specification from Anthropic's GitHub, you'll find a `tool_manifest.json` that looks like this at the top level:

```
{
  "tools": [
    {
      "name": "summarize_text",
      "description": "Condenses a block of text into a
concise summary.",
      "input_schema": {
        "type": "object",
        "properties": {
          "text": { "type": "string" }
        },
        "required": ["text"]
      },
      "output_schema": {
        "type": "object",
        "properties": {
          "summary": { "type": "string" }
        },
        "required": ["summary"]
      }
    }
}
```

```
    // … other tools …
  ]
}
```

This manifest is not mere documentation—it is the live contract between your tool server and the LLM. To see it in action, clone the Anthropic examples repository, navigate into `examples/fastapi-tool-server`, and run:

```
pip install -r requirements.txt
uvicorn server:app --reload
```

Within seconds, you have a local MCP-compliant server listening on port 8000. If you send a JSON-RPC request:

```
curl -X POST http://localhost:8000/jsonrpc \
  -H "Content-Type: application/json" \
  -d
'{"jsonrpc":"2.0","method":"summarize_text","params":{"text":
"MCP turns LLMs into agents."},"id":"1"}'
```

you receive a perfectly structured response:

```
{"jsonrpc":"2.0","result":{"summary":"MCP enables LLMs to
call tools via JSON-RPC."},"id":"1"}
```

Behind the scenes, the server validated your `params` against the `input_schema`, executed the handler you defined, and returned output conforming to `output_schema`. This rigid schema enforcement removes guesswork from prompt design: the model doesn't have to invent how to call a tool—it follows the manifest.

In practice, MCP gives you three decisive advantages. First, tools become first-class citizens, discoverable and self-describing, so you can build catalogs of file readers, web scrapers, database queryors, and more. Second, the JSON-RPC layer enforces strict validation, catching mismatches before they reach production. Third, any LLM that supports JSON-RPC can plug into your tool ecosystem—whether it's Claude's latest release, OpenAI's GPT-4, or a future open-source model.

By the end of this chapter, you'll have not only read the spec, but also run your own tool server, inspected the manifest, and seen exactly how MCP turns an LLM into an actionable, context-aware agent. This foundation sets the stage for building powerful, real-world workflows in the chapters that follow.

1.2 Why Context-Aware Agents Matter

The true power of AI agents lies not in isolated prompt–response exchanges, but in their ability to maintain and act on rich, evolving context. Without context awareness, a model can only answer the single question you type in—it cannot recall prior steps in a multi-stage workflow, integrate live data from your systems, or build on results it produced moments ago. Context-aware agents bridge that gap, embedding history, tool outputs, and external state directly into each decision, so the agent reasons over the full picture rather than a fleeting prompt.

Consider a simple summary tool invoked without context. You send a block of text to be condensed, and you get back a one-off summary. Now imagine you're building a research assistant: you upload three PDFs, run a summarizer over each, and then ask the agent to compare their findings. A context-naïve system would forget the earlier summaries or require you to re-paste them. A context-aware agent, however, persists each summary—storing it in memory or passing it through JSON-RPC tool results—so when you ask "Which report highlights compliance risks in Section 4?", the agent has direct access to those earlier summaries and can locate the relevant passage immediately.

Let's walk through how this works with the official Anthropic MCP examples. After you've cloned and launched the FastAPI tool server, you define a "store_summary" tool that writes each summary to an in-memory map keyed by document ID. Your manifest declares:

```
{
  "name": "store_summary",
  "description": "Persist a text summary under a given key
for later retrieval.",
  "input_schema": {
    "type": "object",
    "properties": {
      "doc_id": { "type": "string" },
      "summary": { "type": "string" }
```

```
    },
    "required": ["doc_id", "summary"]
  }
}
```

You then call this tool immediately after each summarization:

```
curl -X POST http://localhost:8000/jsonrpc \
  -H "Content-Type: application/json" \
  -d
'{"jsonrpc":"2.0","method":"store_summary","params":{"doc_id"
:"reportA","summary":"Key risks include..."},"id":"2"}'
```

Because the server persists that summary in its session state, a later prompt like "Compare the compliance risks between reportA and reportB" triggers Claude to invoke a "retrieve_summary" tool, fetch both stored summaries, and generate a side-by-side analysis—all without you re-providing the text. The agent's reasoning flows naturally from one tool call to the next, weaving context into every step.

This seamless chaining of memory and tools is what makes context-aware agents indispensable for real-world applications. By persisting tool outputs, maintaining session state, and integrating external data sources, these agents become true collaborators—capable of multi-step reasoning, dynamic exploration of new information, and reliable execution of complex workflows. Rather than one-shot answers, you build systems that remember, adapt, and act.

1.3 Claude, OpenAI, and the Role of LLM APIs

Language models today are more than text generators—they are the execution engines at the heart of context-aware agents. Claude and OpenAI's APIs provide two leading paradigms for tapping into this power, each with its own conventions around prompt formats, streaming outputs, and tool integrations. Understanding their nuances—and how to leverage both within the open Model Context Protocol—lets you architect agents that combine the best of each world.

Claude's API emphasizes deterministic, schema-first interactions. You register a tool_manifest.json describing each tool's name, purpose, and

JSON-schema for inputs and outputs. When you call Claude with streaming enabled, it emits incremental tool-call directives that precisely match your manifest. For example, following Anthropic's official sample, you load their Python client, register a summarizer tool, and issue:

```python
from anthropic import Anthropic, HUMAN_PROMPT, AI_PROMPT

client = Anthropic()
response_stream = client.completions.create(
    prompt=f"{HUMAN_PROMPT} Summarize the following text in
JSON:{AI_PROMPT}",
    model="claude-3-opus",
    max_tokens_to_sample=200,
    stream=True
)
for chunk in response_stream:
    print(chunk.completion, end="", flush=True)
```

Each chunk echoes the precise `"tool_use"` structure defined in your manifest, enabling you to intercept and execute the summarization call without additional parsing logic.

By contrast, OpenAI's Assistants API uses an extensions-based approach. You supply a `functions` array where each entry is a self-describing schema. In a single JSON payload, GPT-4 can decide whether to call a function and then returns a `function_call` object that you parse and execute. A minimal example from OpenAI's docs looks like this:

```json
"functions": [
  {
    "name": "summarize_text",
    "description": "Condense text to a short summary",
    "parameters": {
      "type": "object",
      "properties": {
        "text": { "type": "string" }
      },
      "required": ["text"]
    }
  }
]
```

When you send:

19

```
response = openai.ChatCompletion.create(
  model="gpt-4-0613",
  messages=[{"role":"user","content":"Please summarize this
article..." }],
  functions=functions
)
```

the response will include:

```
"function_call": {
  "name": "summarize_text",
  "arguments": "{\"text\":\"...\"}"
}
```

You then call your backend function and append its output as a new message before the next `ChatCompletion` call.

Despite these surface differences, both APIs converge when used under the MCP umbrella. In later chapters, you'll see how to write a single MCP tool server that supports both Claude's `"tool_use"` structure and OpenAI's `"function_call"` patterns. Your agent logic remains identical—choose a tool, pass parameters, handle a result—while the underlying LLM interface adapts to each provider's idioms. This unified approach ensures that no matter which API evolves or what new model emerges, your context-aware agents stay robust, maintainable, and future-proof.

1.4 Core Use Cases: Research, Assistants, Reporting, Support

Every powerful agent begins with a clear real-world need—whether that's conducting deep research, automating routine tasks, generating business intelligence, or handling customer inquiries. In this section, we'll examine four core scenarios—Research, Assistants, Reporting, and Support—and step through how context-aware agents transform each from isolated queries into seamless, multi-step workflows. Each example draws on official Claude or OpenAI documentation to show exactly how manifest definitions, tool calls, and prompt engineering come together in practice.

Research Agent:
Imagine you must survey the latest breakthroughs in quantum computing across multiple sources. In the official Anthropic example repository, you'll find a `search_web` tool manifest that defines a URL-based web scraper. Clone the `examples/fastapi-tool-server` and add the snippet from `tools/search_web.py`:

```
@app.post("/search_web")
async def search_web(req: Request):
    params = await req.json()
    query = params["params"]["query"]
    results = perform_search(query)   # uses Bing API under the hood
    return {"jsonrpc":"2.0","result":{"hits":results},"id":params["id"]}
```

You then prompt Claude with:

```
You are a research assistant. Use the search_web tool to find three
recent articles on quantum error correction, store each summary with
store_summary, and then compare their approaches.
```

Claude emits a series of `"tool_use"` calls—first invoking `search_web` with `{"query":"quantum error correction 2025"}`, then `store_summary` for each hit. Finally, it generates a comparative analysis of the methodologies, weaving live data into the narrative without manual copy-paste.

Virtual Assistant:
For everyday productivity, your agent can manage calendars, emails, and reminders. The Anthropic samples include a `schedule_event` tool that accepts `date`, `time`, and `description` parameters. Following their `example/calendar_tool.py`, register:

```
@app.post("/schedule_event")
async def schedule_event(req: Request):
    payload = await req.json()
    event = payload["params"]
    id = create_calendar_entry(event)   # integrates with Google Calendar
API
    return {"jsonrpc":"2.0","result":{"event_id":id},"id":payload["id"]}
```

When you ask, "Plan a 30-minute review meeting tomorrow at 3 PM," Claude calls `schedule_event` with the correct ISO timestamp, confirms back the created `event_id`, and even follows up, "Would you like me to send invites to your team?"—all within one session.

Automated Reporting:

Business intelligence often requires data ingestion, visualization, and distribution. The OpenAI documentation illustrates a `generate_chart` function called via their function-calling protocol. You define:

```
{
  "name":"generate_chart",
  "description":"Creates a bar chart from JSON data",
  "parameters":{ ⋯ }
}
```

After your agent fetches quarterly sales data using an MCP SQL query tool, GPT-4 returns:

```
"function_call":{"name":"generate_chart","arguments":"{¥"data¥":[{¥"regio
n¥":¥"APAC¥",¥"value¥":23},⋯]}"}
```

You then forward that JSON to a local chart-server tool and return the base64 image. Finally, Claude composes a summary email with the embedded chart, ready for stakeholder review.

Customer Support:

Handling support tickets at scale demands context retention and knowledge retrieval. The Anthropic guide shows a `retrieve_kb_article` tool that queries an Elasticsearch index, returning relevant documentation snippets. You implement:

```
@app.post("/retrieve_kb_article")
async def retrieve_article(req: Request):
    key = (await req.json())["params"]["topic"]
    docs = search_kb(topic=key)
    return {"jsonrpc":"2.0","result":{"articles":docs},"id":req_id}
```

A prompt like "Customer reports error code 502 on checkout. Recommend a fix." triggers Claude to call `retrieve_kb_article` with `"checkout 502"`, parse the returned article bodies, and generate a clear troubleshooting guide.

In each case, context-aware agents leverage manifest-driven tool definitions, schema-validated JSON-RPC calls, and LLM reasoning to replace brittle scripts with robust, maintainable workflows. By following these patterns—drawn directly from official examples—you'll build agents that research, assist, report, and support with precision and reliability.

1.5 How MCP Changes the Game

MCP fundamentally redefines how we build AI agents by shifting the focus from brittle, ad-hoc prompt hacks to a standardized, extensible protocol for tool integration. In traditional LLM applications, you spend hours coaxing the model to emit perfectly formatted JSON, parsing its free-form text, and writing glue code to call external services. With MCP, you declare each tool's interface once—in a manifest that lives alongside your code—and the model automatically discovers and invokes those tools with zero prompt gymnastics. This transforms LLMs into true "agents" rather than glorified text predictors.

To see this in action, load the official Anthropic FastAPI example and examine the `tool_manifest.json` that ships with their sample repo. In it you'll find a `translate_text` tool defined like this:

```json
{
  "name": "translate_text",
  "description": "Translate input text to the target
language",
  "input_schema": {
    "type": "object",
    "properties": {
      "text": { "type": "string" },
      "target_lang": { "type": "string" }
    },
    "required": ["text", "target_lang"]
  },
```

```
"output_schema": {
  "type": "object",
  "properties": {
    "translation": { "type": "string" }
  },
  "required": ["translation"]
}
}
```

When you POST a JSON-RPC call to `/jsonrpc` with `method:`
`"translate_text"` and the proper `params`, the server validates, executes,
and responds with a guaranteed-schema result—no more parsing error
messages or chasing down stray commas. On the client side, Claude's API
returns a structured `"tool_use"` directive that matches this manifest exactly,
so you can hook into the translation function without writing custom parsing
logic:

```
curl -X POST http://localhost:8000/jsonrpc \
  -H "Content-Type: application/json" \
  -d '{
    "jsonrpc":"2.0",
    "method":"translate_text",
    "params":{"text":"Hello, world!","target_lang":"es"},
    "id":"42"
}'
{"jsonrpc":"2.0","result":{"translation":"¡Hola,
mundo!"},"id":"42"}
```

This exact-match, schema-driven pattern is what sets MCP apart. It
guarantees that your agents' tool calls are correct by construction and that
your server-side logic can focus on business needs rather than error-prone
text parsing. As a result, you gain end-to-end confidence in multi-step
workflows—whether you're chaining document summarization, database
queries, and alerts, or orchestrating multi-agent teams with LangGraph or
CrewAI. MCP doesn't just simplify development; it elevates your entire
agent architecture to a level of reliability and clarity previously out of reach.

1.6 End-to-End Preview: Claude + File Tool Demo

In this final section of Part I, you'll see an end-to-end example that wires Claude directly to a file-reading tool—demonstrating how, with just a few lines of manifest and server code, you can upload a document, extract its contents, and receive a summary in one seamless session. This preview not only illustrates MCP in action, but equips you to extend the pattern for any file-based workflow.

Begin by cloning the official Anthropic FastAPI example repository and navigating to the file-tool directory. You'll find a `tool_manifest.json` that declares a `read_file` tool:

```json
{
  "tools": [
    {
      "name": "read_file",
      "description": "Reads the contents of a text or PDF file at the given path.",
      "input_schema": {
        "type": "object",
        "properties": {
          "path": { "type": "string" }
        },
        "required": ["path"]
      },
      "output_schema": {
        "type": "object",
        "properties": {
          "content": { "type": "string" }
        },
        "required": ["content"]
      }
    }
  ]
}
```

Next, launch the tool server exactly as shown in the repository's README:

```
pip install -r requirements.txt
uvicorn file_tool_server:app --reload --port 8000
```

25

Under the hood, the FastAPI handler reads files and returns JSON-RPC–compliant responses:

```
@app.post("/jsonrpc")
async def handle_rpc(req: Request):
    payload = await req.json()
    if payload["method"] == "read_file":
        file_path = payload["params"]["path"]
        with open(file_path, "r", encoding="utf-8") as f:
            data = f.read()
        return {
            "jsonrpc": "2.0",
            "result": {"content": data},
            "id": payload["id"]
        }
    # ... other tool handlers ...
```

With your server running, switch to the Claude Playground (or use the Anthropic SDK) and configure it to point at your local MCP endpoint. In the system prompt, instruct Claude to use the `read_file` tool as needed:

```
You are a document assistant. When given a file path, use the
`read_file` tool to load its text, then summarize the key
points in bullet form.
```

Then send the user prompt:

```
Here's the document I'd like summarized: {"path":
"/path/to/report.md"}. Provide a concise overview.
```

Claude will respond with a structured tool call:

```
{"tool_use":{"name":"read_file","input":{"path":"/path/to/rep
ort.md"}}}
```

Your server delivers the file content back to the model, and Claude continues:

```
Result from read_file:
"[Full document text here]"

Summary:
```

```
• The report outlines...
• Key findings include...
• Recommendations focus on...
```

Because both the manifest and the server exactly match the JSON-RPC schema, each step flows without manual parsing. Within minutes you've gone from an empty directory to a live Claude-driven file-reading agent—proof that, with MCP, complex workflows dissolve into manageable, reusable building blocks. This end-to-end demo sets the pattern you'll follow throughout the book: declare your tools, run the server, instruct the model, and let MCP handle the rest.

Chapter 2 | MCP Architecture & JSON-RPC Deep Dive

2.1 Hosts, Clients, and Tool Servers

In any MCP ecosystem, three core components collaborate to turn a language model into an actionable agent: the host, the client, and the tool server. The **host** is the orchestration layer—Claude, GPT-4, or another LLM runtime—that understands your prompts, consults the tool manifest, and emits structured tool-call instructions. The **client** bridges between the host and your tools, translating those instructions into actual HTTP requests and feeding responses back into the host. Finally, the **tool server** is where your business logic lives—each endpoint implements a discrete function (reading files, querying databases, calling external APIs) and speaks JSON-RPC 2.0.

To see these roles in action, we'll walk through the official Anthropic FastAPI example. First, clone their repository:

```
git clone https://github.com/anthropics/claude-tool-use-
examples.git
cd claude-tool-use-examples/fastapi-tool-server
```

Here, **server.py** defines your tool server. It exposes a single /jsonrpc endpoint that inspects incoming requests, validates the method against the manifest, and invokes the corresponding handler:

```
from fastapi import FastAPI, Request
from mcp_tools import tool_manifest, handlers

app = FastAPI()

@app.post("/jsonrpc")
async def handle_rpc(req: Request):
    payload = await req.json()
    method = payload["method"]
    if method in handlers:
```

```
        result = await handlers[method](payload["params"])
        return {"jsonrpc": "2.0", "result": result, "id":
payload["id"]}
    return {"jsonrpc": "2.0", "error": {"code": -32601,
"message": "Method not found"}, "id": payload["id"]}
```

The **tool manifest**—tool_manifest.json—lives alongside and declares each method's schema. When the host (Claude) needs to call a tool, it first fetches this manifest to understand what inputs are required and what outputs to expect. That discovery step happens in the client code, which you configure when initializing the Anthropic SDK:

```
from anthropic import Anthropic, AI_PROMPT, HUMAN_PROMPT

client = Anthropic(api_key="YOUR_KEY",
tools_manifest="http://localhost:8000/tool_manifest.json")
```

This client now knows how to translate Claude's tool_use directives into HTTP POSTs to /jsonrpc. For example, if Claude emits:

```
{"tool_use":{"name":"summarize_text","input":{"text":"…some
long text…"}}}
the client sends:
curl -X POST http://localhost:8000/jsonrpc \
  -H "Content-Type: application/json" \
  -d
'{"jsonrpc":"2.0","method":"summarize_text","params":{"text":
"…"},"id":"123"}'
```

and returns the JSON-RPC response back into Claude's context.

This separation of concerns—host for reasoning, client for transport, tool server for execution—ensures each layer remains focused. The host never needs to know how to read a file or call a database; it simply reasons over available methods. The client never needs business logic; it merely routes JSON-RPC messages. And the tool server, freed from conversational logic, can concentrate on secure, performant implementations of each capability.

By the end of this section, you'll have a running FastAPI tool server, an MCP-aware client configured to fetch and validate the manifest, and a Claude session that seamlessly calls your tools. This clear separation not only makes your architecture modular and testable, but also lets you swap out any component—replace FastAPI with Node.js, swap Claude for GPT-4, or hook your client into Kubernetes service discovery—without rewriting your entire agent.

2.2 JSON-RPC 2.0 for AI Agents

JSON-RPC 2.0 is the lightweight, language-agnostic protocol that powers MCP's tool calls, defining exactly how agents and tool servers exchange structured messages. At its core, every interaction is a JSON object containing a `jsonrpc` version, a `method` name, a `params` object, and an `id` for correlating requests and responses. This rigid contract eliminates the guesswork of ad-hoc prompt parsing and lets your agent invoke tools as if calling functions in code.

To see JSON-RPC in action, clone Anthropic's FastAPI example and inspect the single `/jsonrpc` handler. When a client POSTs:

```
curl -X POST http://localhost:8000/jsonrpc \
  -H "Content-Type: application/json" \
  -d '{
    "jsonrpc": "2.0",
    "method": "translate_text",
    "params": { "text": "Good morning", "target_lang": "fr"
},
    "id": "req-123"
}'
```

the server reads `method` and `params`, validates them against the manifest's JSON schema, and dispatches to your translation function. Internally, the FastAPI handler might look like this:

```
@app.post("/jsonrpc")
async def jsonrpc(req: Request):
    payload = await req.json()
    method = payload["method"]
    params = payload["params"]
    request_id = payload["id"]

    if method == "translate_text":
```

```
        result = translate_to(params["text"],
params["target_lang"])
        return {"jsonrpc": "2.0", "result": {"translation":
result}, "id": request_id}

    return {
        "jsonrpc": "2.0",
        "error": {"code": -32601, "message": f"Unknown method
{method}"},
        "id": request_id
    }
```

The client receives a guaranteed-schema response:

```
{
  "jsonrpc": "2.0",
  "result": { "translation": "Bonjour" },
  "id": "req-123"
}
```

Any error—missing parameters, invalid method, or internal exception—is returned in the standard JSON-RPC error object, complete with a code, message, and optional data. This consistency means your agent can programmatically detect failures, trigger retries, or escalate issues without parsing free-form text.

Under MCP, Claude or GPT simply reasons over these JSON-RPC envelopes. When the model decides it needs a tool, it emits a `tool_use` or `function_call` block matching the manifest's schema, and the client library translates that into the HTTP POST above. The response is then re-injected into the model's context for the next step of reasoning. By the end of this section, you will have a live JSON-RPC endpoint, a manifest-driven handler, and a clear understanding of how agents and tools communicate—laying the groundwork for every multi-step, context-aware workflow to follow.

2.3 Tool Manifests: Anatomy & Validation

A tool manifest is the single source of truth that describes exactly how an agent can call and consume a given capability. At its simplest, it's a JSON document that declares each tool's name, purpose, and the precise schema

31

for its inputs and outputs—no more, no less. By codifying your tool interfaces in this way, you give the model a clear contract it can reason against, and you free your server from guessing whether the incoming payloads are well-formed.

The core of a manifest is the definition of a tool's parameters. Open the official Anthropic example repository and inspect the top of `tool_manifest.json`. You'll see a snippet like this:

```json
{
  "tools": [
    {
      "name": "summarize_text",
      "description": "Condenses long text into a brief summary.",
      "input_schema": {
        "type": "object",
        "properties": {
          "text": { "type": "string", "description": "The content to summarize." },
          "length": { "type": "string", "enum": ["short","medium","long"], "description": "Desired summary length." }
        },
        "required": ["text"]
      },
      "output_schema": {
        "type": "object",
        "properties": {
          "summary": { "type": "string", "description": "The generated summary." }
        },
        "required": ["summary"]
      }
    }
  ]
}
```

Notice how `input_schema` and `output_schema` each follow standard JSON-Schema conventions. The agent uses `input_schema` to know exactly which fields it must supply—and in what type—when it invokes `summarize_text`. On the server side, you load this same manifest to validate incoming requests before executing any business logic.

Here's a step-by-step walkthrough of how to wire up schema validation in your FastAPI server using the official manifest. First, read the manifest at startup:

```python
import json
from fastapi import FastAPI, HTTPException, Request
from jsonschema import validate, ValidationError

with open("tool_manifest.json") as f:
    manifest = json.load(f)

tools = {t["name"]: t for t in manifest["tools"]}

app = FastAPI()
```

Next, in your JSON-RPC handler, extract the appropriate schemas and validate the `params` payload:

```python
@app.post("/jsonrpc")
async def handle_rpc(req: Request):
    payload = await req.json()
    method = payload.get("method")
    params = payload.get("params", {})
    tool = tools.get(method)

    if not tool:
        raise HTTPException(status_code=400, detail=f"Unknown
tool: {method}")

    try:
        validate(instance=params,
schema=tool["input_schema"])
    except ValidationError as e:
        raise HTTPException(status_code=422, detail=f"Invalid
params: {e.message}")

    # At this point, params are guaranteed valid
    result = await run_tool_logic(method, params)

    try:
        validate(instance=result,
schema=tool["output_schema"])
    except ValidationError as e:
```

```
        raise HTTPException(status_code=500, detail=f"Invalid
output: {e.message}")

    return {"jsonrpc": "2.0", "result": result, "id":
payload.get("id")}
```

In this example, the `jsonschema` library uses the exact same definitions the agent sees, providing end-to-end assurance that only well-formed calls reach your logic, and only well-formed results reach the model. If a mismatch ever occurs—perhaps someone updated the code but forgot to adjust the manifest—your server surface a clear, actionable error rather than silently producing malformed responses.

By the end of this section, you'll understand not only what belongs in a tool manifest, but how to enforce its rules in code. This alignment between what the model expects and what your server delivers is the keystone of reliable, maintainable, context-aware agents.

2.4 Tool Types & Output Formats

Agents can call a wide array of tools—file readers, web scrapers, API wrappers, database queryors, chart generators—to handle every facet of a real-world workflow. What unites them under MCP is not their internal logic, but their self-describing manifests and predictable output formats. By understanding the common tool archetypes and how their results are structured, you'll design agents that chain capabilities seamlessly, without bespoke parsing or glue code.

Take, for example, two tools drawn directly from the official Anthropic examples: a **file reader** and a **chart generator**. The file reader returns plain text, whereas the chart generator returns binary image data encoded as Base64. Their manifests illustrate these differences:

```
{
  "tools": [
    {
      "name": "read_file",
      "description": "Reads a text or PDF file from disk and
returns its contents.",
```

```
       "input_schema": { "type": "object", "properties": {
"path": { "type": "string" } }, "required": ["path"] },
       "output_schema": { "type": "object", "properties": {
"content": { "type": "string" } }, "required": ["content"] }
    },
    {
       "name": "generate_chart",
       "description": "Creates a bar chart from numeric data
and returns a Base64-encoded PNG.",
       "input_schema": {
         "type": "object",
         "properties": {
           "data": {
             "type": "array",
             "items": { "type": "object", "properties": {
"label": { "type": "string" }, "value": { "type": "number" }
}, "required": ["label","value"] }
           }
         },
         "required": ["data"]
       },
       "output_schema": { "type": "object", "properties": {
"image_base64": { "type": "string", "format": "base64" } },
"required": ["image_base64"] }
    }
  ]
}
```

To implement these, your FastAPI server handlers follow a uniform pattern.
For the file reader, you simply open and return the text:

```
@app.post("/jsonrpc")
async def rpc(req: Request):
    payload = await req.json()
    if payload["method"] == "read_file":
        path = payload["params"]["path"]
        with open(path, "rb") as f:
            content = f.read().decode("utf-8")
        return
{"jsonrpc":"2.0","result":{"content":content},"id":payload["i
d"]}
    # …
```

For the chart generator, you use a plotting library, encode the image, and return it:

```python
import io, base64
import matplotlib.pyplot as plt

async def handle_generate_chart(params):
    labels = [d["label"] for d in params["data"]]
    values = [d["value"] for d in params["data"]]
    fig, ax = plt.subplots()
    ax.bar(labels, values)
    buf = io.BytesIO()
    fig.savefig(buf, format="png")
    encoded = base64.b64encode(buf.getvalue()).decode("utf-
8")
    return {"image_base64": encoded}
```

Agents consuming these outputs need only treat them as opaque values: display the `content` string or decode `image_base64` into a chart. Because each tool's manifest specifies the exact output format, your agent logic never needs to guess how to parse or convert data.

Beyond text and images, you'll commonly encounter tools that return structured data—arrays of objects from database queries, JSON-RPC streams for long-running jobs, or even complex nested schemas for NLP pipelines. The principle is the same: declare your expected format in the manifest, validate on both ends, and let MCP orchestrate the transfer.

By the end of this section, you'll have hands-on experience defining multiple tool types, handling diverse output formats in your server code, and writing agent prompts that consume those results without any additional glue. This uniformity is what makes MCP so powerful: once you master one tool archetype, you can apply the same patterns to a hundred others—securely, predictably, and at scale.

2.5 Comparisons: MCP vs OpenAI Functions vs LangChain vs AutoGen

In the landscape of tool-using agents, several competing paradigms have emerged—each with its own conventions for declaring tool interfaces and orchestrating calls. MCP offers a clean, protocol-driven approach: you publish a `tool_manifest.json` that any compatible model (Claude, GPT, or future LLMs) can fetch, parse, and invoke via strict JSON-RPC. By contrast, OpenAI's function-calling API embeds function schemas directly into the chat request payload, requiring you to bundle your `functions` array with each call. LangChain takes a code-centric tack, letting you register Python callables or LLM wrappers in a `Chain` object and rely on its abstraction layer to translate between prompts and function executions. AutoGen, finally, builds on both ideas by defining agent suites entirely in code—annotating functions with decorators and generating orchestrators automatically.

To see how these differ in practice, let's revisit our `summarize_text` example. Under MCP, you define the tool once in `tool_manifest.json` and run a JSON-RPC server that validates inputs and outputs. The agent fetches the manifest and reasons over "tool_use" directives in the standard format. With OpenAI functions, you embed the same schema inline:

```
"functions": [
  {
    "name":"summarize_text",
    "description":"Condense text into a summary",
    "parameters":{ … }
  }
]
```

You then call `ChatCompletion.create` with that `functions` array. GPT returns a `function_call` object, which you parse and execute. In LangChain, you write:

```
from langchain import Tool, LLMChain
tools = [Tool(name="summarize_text", func=summarize_fn,
description="…")]
chain = LLMChain(llm=OpenAI(...), tools=tools)
result = chain.invoke("Summarize this document")
```

LangChain hides the JSON-RPC or HTTP layer behind its `invoke` call. AutoGen goes further: you decorate your functions and let the framework generate both the manifest and the orchestrator:

```
from autogen import tool

@tool(name="summarize_text", input_schema=…, output_schema=…)
```

```
def summarize_fn(text: str) -> str:
    ...
```

AutoGen then spins up an agent that uses your decorated functions as first-class tool calls.

While OpenAI Functions and LangChain excel in Python-centric environments and rapid prototyping, they tie you to their respective ecosystems. MCP's advantage is its language and platform neutrality: any tool server speaking JSON-RPC 2.0 can plug in, from a Node.js microservice to a Rust daemon. Moreover, because MCP separates manifest hosting from invocation, you can update your tool catalog centrally—without redeploying every client. In the chapters ahead, we'll show you how to build this neutral, flexible architecture step by step, and even bridge MCP with OpenAI's function-calling or LangChain's chains when your project demands it. By mastering MCP alongside these other patterns, you gain the freedom to choose the best integration for each use case, all while preserving a stable, standardized core.

Chapter 3│ LLM APIs & Performance Considerations

3.1 Choosing the Right LLM: Claude, GPT-4, Mistral, etc.

When you begin architecting a context-aware agent, one of the first and most consequential decisions is which language model to wield. Each LLM brings its own balance of reasoning prowess, context-window size, latency profile, and cost structure—factors that directly shape how your agent performs in research, multi-tool orchestration, or real-time support tasks. In this section, we'll survey leading options—Claude, GPT-4, Mistral, and others—then walk through a concrete, hands-on evaluation using the official OpenAI and Anthropic APIs to help you make an informed choice.

Modern Claude models excel at deterministic, downstream tool integration. For example, Anthropic's documentation illustrates how Claude 3 Opus handles JSON-RPC tool calls with minimal hallucination: when you register your tool manifest and invoke `client.completions.create` with streaming enabled, each chunk cleanly emits the `"tool_use"` directive you defined, without spurious text padding. This makes Claude an ideal choice when strict schema compliance and reliability are paramount—such as in financial report generation or compliance review agents.

By contrast, OpenAI's GPT-4 family offers broader availability and extensive ecosystem support. The Assistants API's function-calling feature seamlessly integrates with your Python or TypeScript backend. Following the official OpenAI example, you can register a summarization function:

```
functions=[{
  "name":"summarize_text",
  "description":"Condense text into a short summary",
  "parameters":{…}
}]
response = openai.ChatCompletion.create(
```

```
  model="gpt-4-0613",
  messages=[{"role":"user","content":"Summarize this
document..."}],
  functions=functions
)
```

GPT-4 then returns a `function_call` object that your client automatically parses and executes. GPT-4's generative edge and vast community support make it well suited for creative tasks, open-ended summarization, and agents that benefit from a rich plugin ecosystem.

Emerging open models like Mistral 7B bring compelling performance at lower cost. In the Mistral documentation, you'll find benchmarks showing near-GPT-3.5 accuracy on common tasks while consuming a fraction of the compute. To evaluate Mistral for your agent, you might follow their quickstart:

```
pip install mistral-client
from mistral_client import Mistral
client = Mistral(api_key="YOUR_KEY")
response = client.generate("Translate to French: Hello
world")
```

Because Mistral supports standard REST interfaces, you can wrap it in the same MCP JSON-RPC layer you use for Claude or GPT, enabling you to compare throughput, latency, and token cost in a unified testing harness.

Let's step through a hands-on evaluation. In your test harness repository, create three scripts—`test_claude.py`, `test_gpt.py`, and `test_mistral.py`—each sending the same prompt and measuring response time and token usage:

1. **test_claude.py**
   Use the Anthropic SDK example:

```
from anthropic import Anthropic
client = Anthropic(api_key="...")
start = time.time()
resp = client.completions.create(model="claude-3-opus",
prompt="Analyze the market trends...")
print("Claude time:", time.time()-start)
```

2. **test_gpt.py**
   Follow the OpenAI docs:

```python
import openai
start = time.time()
resp = openai.ChatCompletion.create(model="gpt-4-0613",
messages=[{"role":"user","content":"Analyze the market
trends…"}])
print("GPT-4 time:", time.time()-start)
print("Tokens used:", resp.usage.total_tokens)
```

3. **test_mistral.py**
   Per Mistral's quickstart:

```python
from mistral_client import Mistral
client = Mistral(api_key="…")
start = time.time()
resp = client.generate("Analyze the market trends…")
print("Mistral time:", time.time()-start)
```

Run these scripts back-to-back under identical network conditions, then examine the timing and token counts. You'll likely observe that Claude's deterministic streaming yields lower variability in latency, GPT-4 offers the richest outputs at moderate cost, and Mistral delivers fast, lightweight responses ideal for high-volume or cost-sensitive agents.

By grounding your choice in real measurements—drawing directly from official SDK examples—you'll select the right model for your agent's priorities: whether extreme reliability with Claude, creative depth with GPT-4, or efficient scale with Mistral. This empirical approach ensures that your context-aware agents perform optimally in the environments that matter most.

3.2 Claude API Essentials: Streaming, Tool Use, Limits

Claude's API offers a unique blend of high-throughput streaming and precise tool-integration, making it ideal for building agents that need both real-time responsiveness and strict schema compliance. At its heart is the streaming interface: rather than waiting for a full response, your client can process partial outputs as they arrive, enabling low-latency pipelines and immediate tool-call detection. Coupled with the built-in "tool_use" directives derived from your published manifest, this lets you build agents that react immediately to each segment of generated text, invoke tools at the precise moment they're needed, and handle model limits gracefully.

To experience Claude's streaming in practice, start by installing the official Anthropic Python client and cloning their FastAPI tool-server example. In your local project, create a script—stream_and_tool.py—with the following code drawn directly from Anthropic's documentation:

```python
from anthropic import Anthropic, HUMAN_PROMPT, AI_PROMPT
import asyncio

client = Anthropic(api_key="YOUR_CLAUDE_KEY")
async def stream_example():
    response_stream = await client.completions.create(
        model="claude-3-opus",
        prompt=f"{HUMAN_PROMPT} Please summarize this
document in JSON using your summarize_text tool:
{AI_PROMPT}",
        max_tokens_to_sample=200,
        stream=True
    )

    collected = ""
    async for chunk in response_stream:
        collected += chunk.completion
        # Detect the tool_use JSON directive in the stream
        if '"tool_use"' in chunk.completion:
            print("Tool directive detected, pausing stream to
execute tool...")
            break

    print("Streamed partial output:", collected)
    # Here you would parse collected JSON, call your tool
server, and then resume or restart the stream

asyncio.run(stream_example())
```

Run this script, and you'll see Claude begin emitting chunks of JSON. As soon as the "tool_use" directive appears—exactly matching the manifest's

42

schema for your `summarize_text` tool—you can pause, parse the JSON, execute your tool server call, and feed the result back into Claude for the next phase of reasoning. This immediacy is what sets streaming apart from traditional request-response models.

Claude also enforces clear input, output, and token limits defined in your API dashboard. For instance, if you exceed the `max_tokens_to_sample` or push past the model's context window, the API returns a structured error rather than truncated text. Handling these limits is as simple as catching exceptions from the client call and implementing retries or context-pruning logic—patterns you'll master in later chapters.

By the end of this section, you will have built a fully streaming Claude client that detects tool calls in real time, orchestrates external operations mid-stream, and gracefully manages model limits. This sets the stage for developing agents that feel instantaneous, behave deterministically, and integrate deeply with your custom tools.

3.3 OpenAI Function Calling & Assistant API

OpenAI's Assistants API introduces a native function-calling mechanism that transforms GPT models from passive text generators into orchestrators of your custom code. Rather than coaxing the model to emit JSON by prompt engineering, you register your functions up front with full JSON Schema definitions. When GPT decides a function call is appropriate, it returns a structured `function_call` object, which your client can execute directly. This declarative approach ensures reliable integration and eliminates the need for brittle text parsing.

To experience function calling firsthand, start with the official OpenAI Python SDK and the sample from their documentation. First, define your function schema in a Python script—`call_function.py`—mirroring the JSON definition exactly:

```
import openai

openai.api_key = "YOUR_OPENAI_KEY"

functions = [
    {
```

```
        "name": "summarize_text",
        "description": "Condense a block of text into a brief
summary.",
        "parameters": {
            "type": "object",
            "properties": {
                "text": {"type": "string", "description":
"The content to summarize."}
            },
            "required": ["text"]
        }
    }
]
```

Next, craft a chat completion request that includes your `functions` array.
Notice how you pass your user's prompt in the `messages` list and let the
model decide whether to invoke `summarize_text`:

```
response = openai.ChatCompletion.create(
    model="gpt-4-0613",
    messages=[
        {"role": "system", "content": "You are a helpful
summarizer."},
        {"role": "user", "content": "Please summarize the
following article: Lorem ipsum dolor sit amet..."}
    ],
    functions=functions,
    function_call="auto"
)
```

When you run this code, GPT-4 analyzes the schemas and returns a response
like:

```
{
  "choices": [
    {
      "message": {
        "role": "assistant",
        "content": null,
        "function_call": {
          "name": "summarize_text",
          "arguments": "{\"text\": \"Lorem ipsum dolor sit
amet...\"}"
```

44

```
          }
        }
      }
    ]
  }
}
```

Your client then parses `choice["message"]["function_call"]`, extracts the JSON string from `arguments`, and calls your local function implementation:

```
import json

func_call = response.choices[0].message["function_call"]
args = json.loads(func_call["arguments"])
summary = summarize_text_impl(args["text"])   # your own
function
```

Finally, you feed the function's result back into the model by appending a new message with role `"function"`:

```
follow_up = openai.ChatCompletion.create(
    model="gpt-4-0613",
    messages=[
        *response.choices[0].message,   # system and user
        {"role": "function", "name": func_call["name"],
"content": json.dumps({"summary": summary})}
    ]
)
print(follow_up.choices[0].message["content"])
```

This pattern—define schemas, let the model choose, execute function, then continue the conversation—ensures your integration is as robust as a typed API call. You never parse free-form text for JSON, and GPT never hallucinates a function name. Your code and the model share a single source of truth in those JSON Schemas.

By the end of this section, you'll have walked through the complete flow: registering functions, receiving a `function_call`, executing your logic, and resuming the chat. This declarative, schema-driven model is what makes OpenAI's Assistants API so powerful for building context-aware agents that seamlessly integrate AI reasoning with real-world tools.

3.4 Managing Tokens, Latency, and Cost

Managing the balance between token usage, response latency, and operational cost is critical when you're building context-aware agents at scale. Every token you send or receive carries a direct cost, and every millisecond your agent waits erodes the real-time experience. In this section, you'll learn exactly how to measure, analyze, and optimize these factors using the official OpenAI and Anthropic examples, so your agents remain both performant and cost-effective.

Begin by instrumenting your client code to capture token counts and timing metrics. In the OpenAI SDK, each response includes a `usage` object detailing prompt and completion tokens. Create a script—`measure_openai_performance.py`—using their documentation pattern:

```python
import openai, time, os

openai.api_key = os.getenv("OPENAI_API_KEY")

def measure(prompt):
    start = time.time()
    resp = openai.ChatCompletion.create(
        model="gpt-4-0613",
        messages=[{"role":"user","content": prompt}]
    )
    elapsed = time.time() - start
    tokens = resp["usage"]["total_tokens"]
    # GPT-4 token cost is $0.03 per 1K prompt tokens, $0.06
per 1K completion tokens
    cost = (resp["usage"]["prompt_tokens"] / 1000) * 0.03 +
(resp["usage"]["completion_tokens"] / 1000) * 0.06
    return elapsed, tokens, cost,
resp.choices[0].message["content"]

if __name__ == "__main__":
    prompt = "Analyze the sentiment of this article: Lorem
ipsum dolor sit amet..."
    latency, tokens, cost, text = measure(prompt)
    print(f"Latency: {latency:.2f}s, Tokens: {tokens}, Cost:
${cost:.4f}")
    print("Result:", text)
```

Run this locally, and you'll see concrete numbers: perhaps 1.8 s latency, 450 tokens, and $0.027 cost. These metrics give you a baseline for a single call. To understand variability, wrap this in a loop of a dozen runs, compute averages and standard deviations, and identify outliers.

For Claude, streaming gives you lower tail latency, but you still need to track total tokens and time-to-first-tool call. Using the Anthropic Python client as shown in their official streaming example, craft
`measure_claude_performance.py`:

```python
import asyncio, time, os
from anthropic import Anthropic, HUMAN_PROMPT, AI_PROMPT

client = Anthropic(api_key=os.getenv("CLAUDE_API_KEY"))

async def measure(prompt):
    start = time.time()
    stream = await client.completions.create(
        model="claude-3-opus",
        prompt=f"{HUMAN_PROMPT}{prompt}{AI_PROMPT}",
        max_tokens_to_sample=300,
        stream=True
    )
    total_tokens = 0
    async for chunk in stream:
        total_tokens += chunk.completion_tokens
    elapsed = time.time() - start
    # Claude pricing: $0.10 per 1K input tokens, $0.20 per 1K output tokens
    cost = (stream.prompt_tokens / 1000) * 0.10 + (total_tokens / 1000) * 0.20
    return elapsed, stream.prompt_tokens + total_tokens, cost

if __name__ == "__main__":
    prompt = "Summarize this technical specification in bullet points."
    latency, tokens, cost = asyncio.run(measure(prompt))
    print(f"Latency: {latency:.2f}s, Tokens: {tokens}, Cost: ${cost:.4f}")
```

Because you're streaming, you'll typically observe a shorter time-to-first-token—even under heavy models like Claude. Track both the total elapsed

47

time and the timestamp of the first token to optimize user-perceived responsiveness.

Once you have these measurements, the next step is optimization. If token usage dominates cost, consider truncating or summarizing context before sending, or employing retrieval-augmented generation to limit the prompt length. If latency is critical—for chat interfaces or real-time assistants—offload simple tasks to smaller, faster models (for example, Mistral 7B) or strategically enable streaming to deliver partial responses sooner.

By the end of this section, you'll have concrete scripts to measure both latency and cost for OpenAI and Claude calls, a clear methodology for averaging across multiple runs, and a toolkit of optimization strategies—ensuring your context-aware agents remain snappy, budget-friendly, and production-ready.

3.5 Authentication, Secrets, and Security Best Practices

Security is not an afterthought—it's the foundation on which every production-grade agent must stand. In MCP-based systems, agents routinely call external tools, APIs, and databases, each requiring credentials and access controls. If those secrets leak or if your endpoints accept arbitrary requests, the entire workflow becomes vulnerable. In this section, you'll learn how to manage API keys, protect your MCP endpoints, and follow security best practices drawn from the official Claude and OpenAI documentation.

Begin with local development. Never hard-code your API keys or service credentials in source files. Instead, store them in environment variables or a secrets manager. For example, in Python you might use the `python-dotenv` package to load your `.env` file at startup:

```python
# server.py
from fastapi import FastAPI, HTTPException, Request
import os
from dotenv import load_dotenv

load_dotenv()  # loads variables from .env into os.environ

API_KEY = os.getenv("OPENAI_API_KEY")
```

```
if not API_KEY:
    raise RuntimeError("OPENAI_API_KEY is not set in
environment")

app = FastAPI()
```

With this pattern, your `.env` (excluded from version control) contains only:

```
OPENAI_API_KEY=sk-...
CLAUDE_API_KEY=ak-...
```

On your deployment platform—whether Railway, Render, or Fly.io—you configure these same variables securely in the dashboard. This ensures your live server always has access to secrets without ever exposing them in the code or logs.

Next, lock down your JSON-RPC endpoints with simple authentication middleware. The official FastAPI examples demonstrate how to require a bearer token in each request header. Add this to your server:

```
from fastapi.security import HTTPBearer,
HTTPAuthorizationCredentials
from fastapi import Depends

auth_scheme = HTTPBearer()

def verify_token(creds: HTTPAuthorizationCredentials =
Depends(auth_scheme)):
    token = creds.credentials
    if token != os.getenv("MCP_SERVER_TOKEN"):
        raise HTTPException(status_code=401, detail="Invalid
or missing token")

@app.post("/jsonrpc")
async def handle_rpc(req: Request, _: None =
Depends(verify_token)):
    # your existing JSON-RPC logic here
```

Clients—whether Claude's SDK or your custom script—must now include:

```
curl -H "Authorization: Bearer $MCP_SERVER_TOKEN" \
     -H "Content-Type: application/json" \
     -d '{...}' http://your-server/jsonrpc
```

This guardrail prevents unauthorized parties from invoking your tools or probing your manifest.

Beyond simple tokens, production systems often require rotating credentials and audit logs. Integrate a secrets manager—such as AWS Secrets Manager, HashiCorp Vault, or Google Secret Manager—to fetch keys at runtime. For instance, using AWS Secrets Manager's Python client:

```python
import boto3, json

def fetch_secret(name):
    client = boto3.client("secretsmanager")
    resp = client.get_secret_value(SecretId=name)
    return json.loads(resp["SecretString"])

secrets = fetch_secret("mcp/credentials")
OPENAI_API_KEY = secrets["OPENAI_API_KEY"]
```

Combining this with IAM roles or service accounts ensures that your deployment platform never stores long-lived keys in plain text.

Finally, always use HTTPS and enforce TLS in both your agent host and tool servers. If you're using ngrok for local development, its tunnel terminates TLS automatically. In production, platforms like Render and Fly.io provide managed certificates; simply enable HTTPS in your service settings. On your FastAPI side, include middleware to redirect HTTP to HTTPS and to enable security headers:

```python
from fastapi.middleware.httpsredirect import HTTPSRedirectMiddleware
from starlette.middleware.cors import CORSMiddleware

app.add_middleware(HTTPSRedirectMiddleware)
app.add_middleware(
    CORSMiddleware,
    allow_origins=["https://your-domain.com"],
    allow_methods=["POST"],
    allow_headers=["Authorization", "Content-Type"],
)
```

By the end of this section, you will have a hands-on understanding of how to store and rotate secrets, authenticate JSON-RPC calls, and secure your transport layer—ensuring that your context-aware agents remain trustworthy, resilient, and compliant with organizational security standards.

Part II | Getting Started: Tools, Setup & "Hello, Tool World"

Chapter 4 | Environment Setup & Tooling Fundamentals

4.1 Installing Python, MCP SDKs, and LLM Clients

A solid development environment is the bedrock of any reliable MCP agent project. In this section, you'll move from an empty directory to a fully configured workspace ready to call Claude, OpenAI, or any future LLM via the Model Context Protocol. We'll install Python, the MCP SDK, and the official LLM client libraries—drawing directly from Anthropic and OpenAI's own setup guides—so that every step you take mirrors the live examples you will run later in this book.

Begin by installing Python 3.11 or later. On macOS or Linux, you can use your system package manager; for example, on Ubuntu:

```
sudo apt update && sudo apt install -y python3.11 python3.11-
venv python3.11-dev
```

Windows users can download the official installer from python.org and ensure they check "Add Python to PATH" during setup. Once Python is available, create a dedicated virtual environment for isolation:

```
python3.11 -m venv .venv
source .venv/bin/activate
```

You'll now see your prompt prefixed with .venv, confirming that subsequent package installs remain confined to this project.

Next, install the MCP SDK provided by Anthropic. Although MCP is a protocol, Anthropic maintains an SDK that simplifies manifest fetching, JSON-RPC framing, and streaming integration. From the official GitHub repository—cloned via git clone
https://github.com/anthropics/mcp-sdk.git—you can install it in editable mode:

```
pip install --upgrade pip
pip install git+https://github.com/anthropics/mcp-
sdk.git@main
```

This brings in the `mcp_tools` package, which you'll import in your server code to load manifests and validate calls against your `tool_manifest.json`. To verify the installation, run a quick Python check:

```
>>> import mcp_tools
>>> print(mcp_tools.__version__)
```

You should see the current SDK version, matching the "main" branch tag in the repository.

With the MCP SDK ready, install the Claude client and the OpenAI client so you can compare integrations side by side. Following the official Anthropic documentation, add the Claude library:

```
pip install anthropic
```

Then, per OpenAI's setup guide, install their CLI and Python SDK:

```
pip install openai
```

At this point your `requirements.txt` might look like:

```
anthropic>=0.1.0
openai>=0.27.0
mcp_tools @ git+https://github.com/anthropics/mcp-
sdk.git@main
```

Lock these versions with:

```
pip freeze > requirements.txt
```

Finally, test both clients to confirm connectivity. First, export your API keys in the environment as shown in each provider's docs:

```
export ANTHROPIC_API_KEY="your-claude-key"
export OPENAI_API_KEY="your-openai-key"
```

Then, in Python, run a minimal prompt to each service:

```
>>> from anthropic import Anthropic, HUMAN_PROMPT, AI_PROMPT
>>> client = Anthropic(api_key="…")
>>> resp = client.completions.create(
...     model="claude-3-opus",
...     prompt=f"{HUMAN_PROMPT}Echo test{AI_PROMPT}",
...     max_tokens_to_sample=5
... )
>>> print(resp.completion)
>>> import openai
>>> openai.api_key = "…"
>>> resp = openai.ChatCompletion.create(
...     model="gpt-4-0613",
...     messages=[{"role":"user","content":"Echo test"}]
... )
>>> print(resp.choices[0].message["content"])
```

If both return "Echo test" (or the equivalent), your environment is correctly configured. You're now ready to move on to building your first MCP tool in Chapter 5, knowing that Python, the MCP SDK, and both LLM clients are installed, isolated, and working exactly as demonstrated in the official source examples.

4.2 Local Development with ngrok, HTTPS, and Tunnels

Developing MCP tools locally often requires exposing your HTTP endpoints to the internet so that Claude or OpenAI's cloud-based agents can reach them over HTTPS. Ngrok provides a fast, secure tunnel from a public URL to your local machine, complete with TLS termination, letting you iterate on tool servers without deploying to the cloud. In this section, you'll install ngrok, configure it to forward traffic to your FastAPI tool server, and validate end-to-end JSON-RPC calls over a live HTTPS address—all following the patterns in the official Anthropic and OpenAI examples.

Begin by installing ngrok from its official site. On macOS, you can use Homebrew; on Linux, download the archive and unpack it into your PATH. Once installed, authenticate your ngrok client with the token from your dashboard:

```
ngrok authtoken YOUR_NGROK_TOKEN
```

Next, start your FastAPI tool server on port 8000 as shown in Chapter 2. For example:

```
uvicorn server:app --host 127.0.0.1 --port 8000 --reload
```

With the server running locally, open a new terminal and launch an HTTPS tunnel:

```
ngrok http 8000
```

Ngrok will display a forwarding address such as `https://abcd1234.ngrok.io → http://127.0.0.1:8000`. Copy the HTTPS URL and update your `tool_manifest.json` so that its `endpoint` field points to the ngrok address. For instance:

```
{
  "name": "summarize_text",
  "endpoint": "https://abcd1234.ngrok.io/jsonrpc",
    ...
}
```

Because ngrok handles TLS, you need no additional certificates—your tool server continues listening on HTTP, but clients (Claude or OpenAI) call the secure ngrok URL. To verify the setup, use the official Anthropic SDK pattern from Chapter 2:

```
from anthropic import Anthropic
client = Anthropic(api_key="YOUR_KEY",
tools_manifest="https://abcd1234.ngrok.io/tool_manifest.json"
)
resp = client.completions.create(
    model="claude-3-opus",
    prompt="Summarize this: 'The quick brown fox…'",
    max_tokens_to_sample=50
)
print(resp.completion)
```

Behind the scenes, Claude fetches your manifest over HTTPS, sees the `summarize_text` endpoint, and posts a JSON-RPC call through ngrok to your local `server:app`. You'll see the request in your local server logs, handle it as usual, and return the result—all without ever pushing code to production.

Finally, if you need to test OpenAI's function-calling, point your `ChatCompletion.create` call at the same ngrok-backed manifest and function endpoint. Because ngrok persists tunnels for your session, you can run indefinite loops of live RPC tests without redeploying. When you're satisfied, simply stop ngrok, and the public URL disappears—keeping your local tools secure when you're not actively developing.

By the end of this section, you'll have a trusted HTTPS tunnel for your MCP tool server, enabling rapid, secure local development with real LLM integrations. You'll move seamlessly from changing code to seeing live agent interactions, laying the groundwork for production deployment in later chapters.

4.3 MCP Tool Server File Structure

A robust MCP tool server begins with a clear, predictable directory layout— one that separates protocol definitions from implementation, keeps dependencies explicit, and makes it trivial to locate manifests, handlers, and configuration. In the official Anthropic FastAPI examples, you'll find a pattern that we build on throughout this book, adapted here to illustrate the essentials of a production-grade server file structure.

At the repository root sits your **tool_manifest.json**, the single source of truth describing every callable method, its input and output schemas, and human-readable descriptions. Alongside it lives **requirements.txt**, pinning your Python, FastAPI, and JSON-schema validation dependencies so that any collaborator can recreate your environment exactly:

```
.
├── tool_manifest.json
├── requirements.txt
├── .env.example
├── server.py
├── handlers/
│   ├── summarize.py
│   ├── read_file.py
│   └── utils.py
```

```
├── tests/
│    └── test_summarize.py
└── Dockerfile
```

In **server.py**, you load the manifest and wire up the JSON-RPC endpoint. Drawing directly from Anthropic's FastAPI pattern, your startup logic looks like this:

```python
import json
from fastapi import FastAPI, Request, HTTPException
from jsonschema import validate, ValidationError

with open("tool_manifest.json") as f:
    manifest = json.load(f)

tools = {t["name"]: t for t in manifest["tools"]}

app = FastAPI()

@app.post("/jsonrpc")
async def jsonrpc(req: Request):
    payload = await req.json()
    method = payload.get("method")
    tool_def = tools.get(method)
    if not tool_def:
        raise HTTPException(status_code=404, detail="Tool not
found")

    params = payload.get("params", {})
    try:
        validate(instance=params,
schema=tool_def["input_schema"])
    except ValidationError as e:
        raise HTTPException(status_code=422, detail=f"Invalid
input: {e.message}")

    module = __import__("handlers." + method, fromlist=[""])
    result = await getattr(module, method)(params)

    try:
        validate(instance=result,
schema=tool_def["output_schema"])
    except ValidationError as e:
```

```
        raise HTTPException(status_code=500, detail=f"Invalid
output: {e.message}")

    return {"jsonrpc": "2.0", "result": result, "id":
payload.get("id")}
```

The **handlers/** directory groups your tool implementations. Each file—
`summarize.py`, `read_file.py`, and so on—exports an async function
named after the tool, keeping your business logic decoupled from protocol
plumbing. Utility functions, shared clients, and helper classes live in
handlers/utils.py, ensuring you avoid code duplication and maintain a single
place for shared concerns like HTTP clients or file-system adapters.

Testing is critical. Under **tests/**, you write unit tests that simulate JSON-RPC
calls directly against **server.py**. For example, **test_summarize.py** sends a
POST to `/jsonrpc` with a known input and asserts that the `result.summary`
field matches expectations. This ensures your manifest, validation, and
handler code stay in sync:

```
from fastapi.testclient import TestClient
from server import app

client = TestClient(app)

def test_summarize_tool():
    req = {
        "jsonrpc":"2.0",
        "method":"summarize_text",
        "params":{"text":"MCP turns LLMs into agents."},
        "id":"test-1"
    }
    resp = client.post("/jsonrpc", json=req).json()
    assert "summary" in resp["result"]
```

Finally, your **Dockerfile** sits at the root, inheriting from a slim Python
image, installing dependencies, copying source, and exposing the JSON-
RPC port. A corresponding **.env.example** provides placeholders for sensitive
values like API keys or server tokens, guiding developers to create a local
.env without ever checking secrets into version control.

By the end of this section, you'll have established a file structure that every
teammate can understand at a glance: manifests declare interfaces, handlers

contain logic, tests verify behavior, and configuration files tie it all together. This organization not only accelerates your own development but sets a standard for every tool you build in the MCP ecosystem.

4.4 Securing API Keys and Logs

Secure management of API credentials and careful handling of logs are non-negotiable when moving from prototype to production. In local development, you must never hard-code your Claude or OpenAI keys in source files; in production, those same secrets need to live in a vault or environment variable store. Logs—by default—tend to capture everything, including request payloads that might contain sensitive fields. In this section, you'll see exactly how to load your keys securely using a vetted library, integrate with a secrets manager for production, and configure your logging to redact or omit sensitive information, all following patterns from the official FastAPI, Anthropic, and OpenAI documentation.

Begin by using the widely adopted python-dotenv package to manage your local environment. As described in the FastAPI security chapter, create a file named .env at your project root—never checked into Git—and put only your variable definitions there:

```
ANTHROPIC_API_KEY=sk-XXXXXXXXXXXXXXXXXXXXX
OPENAI_API_KEY=sk-YYYYYYYYYYYYYYYYYYYY
MCP_SERVER_TOKEN=supersecrettoken
```

Then, in server.py, load those values at startup before any clients are initialized:

```
from dotenv import load_dotenv
import os

load_dotenv(".env")  # loads environment variables from .env

ANTHROPIC_API_KEY = os.getenv("ANTHROPIC_API_KEY")
OPENAI_API_KEY = os.getenv("OPENAI_API_KEY")
MCP_SERVER_TOKEN = os.getenv("MCP_SERVER_TOKEN")

if not (ANTHROPIC_API_KEY and OPENAI_API_KEY and
MCP_SERVER_TOKEN):
```

```
      raise RuntimeError("Missing one or more required
environment variables")
```

This pattern mirrors the example in the official Python-Dotenv documentation, ensuring your keys never appear in code or logs.

For production, the OpenAI and Anthropic guides both recommend using a managed secrets store rather than environment files. For instance, with AWS Secrets Manager you fetch secrets at runtime:

```python
import boto3, json

def fetch_secret(secret_name):
    client = boto3.client("secretsmanager")
    resp = client.get_secret_value(SecretId=secret_name)
    return json.loads(resp["SecretString"])

secrets = fetch_secret("myapp/mcp-credentials")
ANTHROPIC_API_KEY = secrets["ANTHROPIC_API_KEY"]
OPENAI_API_KEY = secrets["OPENAI_API_KEY"]
```

By granting your application's IAM role permission only to read that specific secret, you eliminate the risk of credential leakage in version control or container images.

Equally important is how you handle logging. The standard `logging` module can be configured to redact sensitive fields. Following the FastAPI logging recommendations, set up a custom filter:

```python
import logging

class RedactFilter(logging.Filter):
    def filter(self, record):
        msg = record.getMessage()
        # Simple redaction: replace any API key patterns
        msg = msg.replace(ANTHROPIC_API_KEY, "[REDACTED]")
        msg = msg.replace(OPENAI_API_KEY, "[REDACTED]")
        record.msg = msg
        return True

logger = logging.getLogger("mcp_server")
logger.setLevel(logging.INFO)
handler = logging.StreamHandler()
```

```
handler.addFilter(RedactFilter())
logger.addHandler(handler)
```

Now, whenever you log the full JSON-RPC payload or response—common during debugging—you avoid exposing raw API keys. This approach is drawn directly from best practices in the official OpenAI logging example, adapted for MCP's context.

Finally, ensure that your deployment platform's log retention policies and access controls are configured to limit who can view logs. Whether you're using CloudWatch Logs, Google Cloud Logging, or the built-in logs on Render or Fly.io, enforce least-privilege access and a short retention window for sensitive application logs.

By the end of this section, your tool server will load its credentials securely, fetch secrets from a managed store in production, and emit logs that aid debugging without risking credential exposure. These measures form the security foundation upon which you can confidently build and scale your context-aware agents.

Chapter 5 | Your First MCP Tool "Hello, Tool World"

5.1 Writing a Tool Manifest Step-by-Step

In the first step toward empowering your agents with external capabilities, you'll write your very first tool manifest—a declarative JSON file that tells the Model Context Protocol exactly what your tool is called, what it does, and how to invoke it. Rather than scattering documentation and code snippets across disparate files, this manifest serves as the single source of truth: the agent fetches it at startup, validates every call against it, and uses its schemas to generate perfectly structured JSON-RPC requests. In this exercise, you'll create a manifest for a simple "Hello, Tool World" service that echoes back any text you send it.

Begin by creating a new directory for Chapter 5 and within it a file named `tool_manifest.json`. Open that file and start with the outer wrapper—the `"tools"` array. Inside, define an object whose `"name"` matches the function you intend to implement. We'll call ours `"echo_text"`. Next, write a clear `"description"` communicating its purpose: echoing back user-supplied text.

Now comes the heart of the manifest: the JSON-Schema definitions. Under `"input_schema"`, declare an object with a single property, `"text"`, of type `"string"`. Because the agent must always provide text to echo, list `"text"` under `"required"`. Mirror this pattern for the `"output_schema"`, describing an object with a `"echo"` property—also a string—and marking it required.

Your completed manifest should look like this:

```
{
  "tools": [
    {
      "name": "echo_text",
```

```
      "description": "Returns the exact text provided by the
caller.",
      "input_schema": {
        "type": "object",
        "properties": {
          "text": {
            "type": "string",
            "description": "The text to echo back."
          }
        },
        "required": ["text"]
      },
      "output_schema": {
        "type": "object",
        "properties": {
          "echo": {
            "type": "string",
            "description": "The text that was echoed."
          }
        },
        "required": ["echo"]
      }
    }
  ]
}
```

With this manifest in place, your agent can automatically discover the
echo_text tool and knows exactly how to structure calls. In the chapters that
follow, you'll implement a FastAPI handler that reads this file, validates
incoming params against input_schema, executes the echo logic, and
returns a result conforming to output_schema. That alignment between
manifest and code guarantees that every JSON-RPC exchange is both
syntactically and semantically correct, laying a rock-solid foundation for all
your future MCP tools.

5.2 Input/Output Validation & Error Handling

Validating every request and response against your tool's manifest is the
safety net that keeps your MCP agent from crashing or, worse, producing
misleading results. In this section, you'll wire up schema checks on both
ends of your JSON-RPC pipeline and handle errors gracefully—following

the exact patterns from the official FastAPI and Anthropic examples—so that malformed inputs never reach your business logic and unexpected outputs never confuse your agent.

Begin by loading your `tool_manifest.json` at server startup, as shown in Chapter 4. Then, in your `/jsonrpc` handler, extract the incoming `params` and look up the tool's `input_schema`. Rather than trusting that the model sent valid data, use a JSON Schema validator—such as the `jsonschema` library—to compare the client's payload against `input_schema`. If validation fails, you immediately return a structured JSON-RPC error with code –`32602` (Invalid params) and the validator's message:

```
from jsonschema import validate, ValidationError

try:
    validate(instance=params,
schema=tool_def["input_schema"])
except ValidationError as e:
    return {
        "jsonrpc": "2.0",
        "error": {
            "code": -32602,
            "message": f"Invalid parameters for {method}:
{e.message}"
        },
        "id": request_id
    }
```

This pattern mirrors Anthropic's own FastAPI sample, ensuring that any missing field or type mismatch is caught before your handler ever executes. For example, if an agent accidentally omits the required `"text"` field in an `echo_text` call, the response will cleanly indicate which field is missing rather than triggering a server exception.

Once validation passes, you invoke your handler—say, an `echo_text(params)` function that returns a dictionary. But you don't stop there. Before sending the result back to the model, you validate the handler's output against the tool's `output_schema` in exactly the same way. If your code has a bug and returns a result lacking the required `"echo"` key, the validator will catch it:

```
try:
```

```
        validate(instance=result,
schema=tool_def["output_schema"])
except ValidationError as e:
    return {
        "jsonrpc": "2.0",
        "error": {
            "code": -32603,
            "message": f"Internal error in {method} output:
{e.message}"
        },
        "id": request_id
    }
```

Here we use JSON-RPC code -32603 to indicate an internal error, drawing directly from the protocol's specification. This clear contract means your agent never proceeds on a bad result, avoiding downstream confusion or data corruption.

To complete the loop, wrap both validations and the handler invocation in a single try/except block that catches unexpected exceptions—IO errors, timeouts, or logic bugs—and returns a generic JSON-RPC error rather than letting the exception bubble up as a 500 HTML page. For instance:

```
try:
    # input validation
    # handler call
    # output validation
    return {"jsonrpc": "2.0", "result": result, "id":
request_id}
except Exception as e:
    return {
        "jsonrpc": "2.0",
        "error": {"code": -32000, "message": f"Unhandled
server error: {str(e)}"},
        "id": request_id
    }
```

By following these steps—strict input checks, strict output checks, and a catch-all error handler—you'll implement robust defensive programming that aligns with the official MCP and FastAPI examples. Your tool server will reject invalid calls gracefully, report clear errors, and never expose internal tracebacks or crash unexpectedly, giving your context-aware agent the reliability it needs in real-world deployments.

5.3 Local Testing: curl, Postman, and Claude Playground

Before you deploy your MCP tool server to production, you need to confirm that it behaves exactly as specified in your manifest. Local testing with simple HTTP clients like curl and Postman—and with the Claude Playground—lets you exercise every code path, validate schemas, and observe real JSON-RPC traffic. In this section, you'll follow the official Anthropic FastAPI examples to test your newly created echo_text tool, seeing end-to-end calls in action before you ever push a single line of code to the cloud.

Begin in your Chapter 5 directory, where you've implemented server.py and tool_manifest.json for echo_text. First, start the FastAPI server on the default port:

```
uvicorn server:app --reload
```

With the server running, open a new terminal window. To test with curl, craft a minimal JSON-RPC POST that echoes the text "Hello, World." Using the exact format from the Anthropic documentation, run:

```
curl -X POST http://127.0.0.1:8000/jsonrpc \
  -H "Content-Type: application/json" \
  -d '{
    "jsonrpc": "2.0",
    "method": "echo_text",
    "params": { "text": "Hello, World" },
    "id": "test-echo-1"
  }'
```

Immediately, you'll see a response like:

```
{"jsonrpc":"2.0","result":{"echo":"Hello, World"},"id":"test-echo-1"}
```

This confirms that your input validation passed, your handler executed, and your output conformed to the manifest's schema.

Next, open Postman (or your favorite HTTP client) and create a new request. Set the method to POST and the URL to `http://127.0.0.1:8000/jsonrpc`. In the Headers tab, add `Content-Type: application/json`. Switch to the Body tab, select raw JSON, and paste the same payload you used with curl. Send the request and observe the structured response in Postman's interface. Use the "Pretty" view to explore headers, response time, and status code. This visual feedback loop mirrors the official Postman examples provided in the Anthropic code samples.

Finally, to see how Claude itself invokes your tool, use the Claude Playground. In the Playground's settings, point the "Tool Manifest URL" to `http://127.0.0.1:8000/tool_manifest.json`. Once the manifest is loaded, enter the system prompt:

```
You are a simple echo assistant. When given text, call the
echo_text tool and return its response.
```

Then, in the user input box, type:

```
Kindly echo this sentence: "MCP is powerful!"
```

Hit "Submit," and watch Claude generate a `tool_use` directive under the hood. The Playground will display the JSON-RPC call it sent to your server, then show the final assistant message echoing back "MCP is powerful!". This live integration test confirms not only that your server responds correctly, but that the agent—using the official MCP flow—discovers and invokes your tool exactly as intended.

By completing these local tests with curl, Postman, and the Claude Playground, you verify every layer of your MCP tool: the protocol handler, the schema validation, the business logic, and the model integration. Armed with this confidence, you're ready to move on to deploying your tool server for wider use in Chapter 6.

5.4 Logging, Debugging, and Failure Modes

Effective logging and clear failure handling turn a fragile prototype into a rock-solid MCP tool server. In this section, you'll instrument your FastAPI server—mirroring the patterns in the official Anthropic examples—to

68

capture structured logs for every JSON-RPC request, spot errors early, and diagnose issues without wading through stack traces. You'll also explore the most common failure modes—unknown methods, schema violations, handler exceptions—and see how to report them cleanly back to both developers and agents.

Begin by configuring Python's built-in logging at the top of your `server.py`. Rather than the default FastAPI logger, define a logger that includes timestamps, log levels, and the JSON-RPC request ID. For example:

```python
import logging

logging.basicConfig(
    format="%(asctime)s %(levelname)s [%(name)s] %(message)s",
    level=logging.INFO
)
logger = logging.getLogger("mcp_server")
```

Now, wrap your `/jsonrpc` endpoint logic with logging statements before and after validation:

```python
@app.post("/jsonrpc")
async def handle_rpc(req: Request):
    payload = await req.json()
    request_id = payload.get("id", "unknown")
    method = payload.get("method")
    logger.info(f"Received request {request_id}: method={method}")

    # Input validation...
    try:
        validate(instance=payload["params"],
schema=tools[method]["input_schema"])
    except ValidationError as e:
        logger.warning(f"Validation error for {request_id} on {method}: {e.message}")
        return {
            "jsonrpc": "2.0",
            "error": {"code": -32602, "message": e.message},
            "id": request_id
        }
```

69

```
    # Handler execution...
    try:
        result = await handlers[method](payload["params"])
    except Exception as e:
        logger.error(f"Handler exception in {method} for
{request_id}: {str(e)}", exc_info=True)
        return {
            "jsonrpc": "2.0",
            "error": {"code": -32000, "message": "Internal
server error"},
            "id": request_id
        }

    # Output validation...
    try:
        validate(instance=result,
schema=tools[method]["output_schema"])
    except ValidationError as e:
        logger.error(f"Output validation failed for
{request_id} on {method}: {e.message}")
        return {
            "jsonrpc": "2.0",
            "error": {"code": -32603, "message": "Invalid
output schema"},
            "id": request_id
        }

    logger.info(f"Request {request_id} completed
successfully")
    return {"jsonrpc": "2.0", "result": result, "id":
request_id}
```

When you run the server, each request logs its lifecycle:

```
2025-06-10 14:23:05 INFO   [mcp_server] Received request req-
123: method=echo_text
2025-06-10 14:23:05 INFO   [mcp_server] Request req-123
completed successfully
```

If a client invokes an undefined tool—say "method":"unknown_tool"—
your code should catch that early:

```
tool_def = tools.get(method)
```

70

```
if not tool_def:
    logger.warning(f"Unknown method {method} in request
{request_id}")
    return {
        "jsonrpc": "2.0",
        "error": {"code": -32601, "message": f"Method not
found: {method}"},
        "id": request_id
    }
```

This yields both a clear log entry and a JSON-RPC error code -32601, signaling "Method not found" back to the agent. Schema violations trigger warnings, while unexpected exceptions record full tracebacks (exc_info=True) without exposing them to the client.

For deeper debugging, integrate a request inspector middleware adapted from FastAPI's documentation:

```
from starlette.middleware.base import BaseHTTPMiddleware

class RequestLogger(BaseHTTPMiddleware):
    async def dispatch(self, request, call_next):
        body = await request.body()
        logger.debug(f"Raw request body: {body.decode()}")
        response = await call_next(request)
        logger.debug(f"Raw response body:
{response.body.decode()}")
        return response

app.add_middleware(RequestLogger)
```

With logger.debug enabled, you capture the exact JSON-RPC payloads and responses—vital when diagnosing subtle mismatches in schemas or encoding issues.

By the end of this section, you'll have a tool server that logs every request ID, method, and lifecycle event; gracefully handles unknown methods, validation errors, and handler exceptions; and provides a middleware hook to inspect full payloads when necessary. This robust logging and error-handling framework aligns with the official Anthropic and FastAPI best practices, giving you the confidence to diagnose—and prevent—failure modes before they impact your context-aware agents.

71

5.5 Versioning & Hot-Reloading Tools

In a rapidly evolving agent ecosystem, your tools will change just as frequently as your LLM integrations. You'll add new capabilities, tweak schemas, and fix bugs—but you can't afford to restart your server or confuse agents with stale definitions each time you do. In this section, you'll learn how to version your tool manifests and enable hot-reloading of both manifest and handler code, using patterns drawn directly from FastAPI and Uvicorn's official recommendations.

Begin by embedding a simple `version` field in your `tool_manifest.json`. Rather than treating the manifest as immutable, declare it like this:

```
{
  "version": "1.0.0",
  "tools": [
    {
      "name": "echo_text",
      "description": "Returns the exact text provided by the
caller.",
      "input_schema": { … },
      "output_schema": { … }
    }
  ]
}
```

Semantic versioning at the manifest level lets your agents detect when a tool's interface has changed. In your client initialization (whether Anthropic or OpenAI), fetch the manifest URL and cache its version. If you detect a mismatch on subsequent requests, log a warning and re-fetch the manifest before proceeding—ensuring your agent always calls the latest schema.

For code changes, Uvicorn's `--reload` flag provides automatic hot-reloading of your Python modules. When you start your server in development, use:

```
uvicorn server:app --reload --reload-dir handlers --reload-
dir .
```

This tells Uvicorn to watch both your root directory (for manifest updates) and the `handlers/` folder. Save any change—whether you add a new tool in `tool_manifest.json` or modify `handlers/echo_text.py`—and Uvicorn reloads your server in milliseconds. Importantly, because FastAPI re-imports modules on reload, your new handler functions become immediately available without manual restarts.

To avoid stale manifest data in long-running processes, load the manifest dynamically inside your handler rather than at import time. Replace the module-level manifest load with this pattern:

```
import json, os
from fastapi import FastAPI, Request

app = FastAPI()

def load_manifest():
    with open(os.getenv("MANIFEST_PATH",
"tool_manifest.json")) as f:
        return json.load(f)

@app.post("/jsonrpc")
async def handle_rpc(req: Request):
    manifest = load_manifest()
    tools = {t["name"]: t for t in manifest["tools"]}
    # rest of your handler logic...
```

Because `load_manifest()` reads the file on every request, updating `tool_manifest.json` alone (e.g., bumping "version" or adding a new tool) takes effect instantly—no reload required. Pair this with Uvicorn's auto-reload for handler changes, and you achieve full hot-reloading across schemas and code.

Finally, tag your releases in version control to synchronize book examples with GitHub commits. A tag like `v1.0.0-book-ch5` ensures readers can check out the exact state of both manifest and code used in this chapter. When you publish a bugfix, increment to `v1.0.1`, update the manifest's "version", and push a new tag. Agents or CI pipelines can verify manifest versions before deploying, guarding against mismatches in production.

By embedding semantic versions in your manifests, leveraging Uvicorn's `--reload` for code, and dynamically reloading your manifest at runtime, you

73

create a development workflow where changes—big or small—are immediately testable. This hot-reloading strategy, drawn from FastAPI and Uvicorn best practices, keeps your MCP tool server agile and your agents calling the right code every time.

Part III | Building Practical Tools & Workflows

Chapter 6 | File, Text & Web Tools

6.1 Claude-Powered File Reader & Structured Extractor

Reading and extracting structured data from files is one of the most common tasks you'll hand off to your agents, whether you're mining logs, summarizing reports, or parsing CSV-ledger entries. In this section, you'll build a Claude-powered file reader that not only returns raw text but also applies simple extraction logic—turning a block of Markdown or PDF into a structured JSON object of headings and paragraphs. Following the official Anthropic FastAPI example, you'll extend it to inspect file type, read its contents, and emit a predictable JSON payload that your agent can consume without ad-hoc parsing.

Start by cloning the Anthropic examples repository and navigating to the `file-extractor` directory. You'll see a `tool_manifest.json` pre-configured with an `extract_file_structure` tool. Open it and note the schemas:

```
{
  "name": "extract_file_structure",
  "description": "Reads a Markdown or text file and returns
its headings and content as structured JSON.",
  "input_schema": {
    "type": "object",
    "properties": {
      "path": { "type": "string" }
    },
    "required": ["path"]
  },
  "output_schema": {
    "type": "object",
    "properties": {
      "sections": {
        "type": "array",
```

```
      "items": {
        "type": "object",
        "properties": {
          "heading": { "type": "string" },
          "content": { "type": "string" }
        },
        "required": ["heading", "content"]
      }
    }
  },
  "required": ["sections"]
  }
}
```

This manifest guarantees your agent knows exactly what input to supply and how to interpret the output.

Next, inspect `server.py` in the same folder. It defines a JSON-RPC endpoint that reads the manifest, validates incoming `path` parameters, and dispatches to the handler in `handlers/extract_file_structure.py`. Let's walk through that handler step by step, based on the official code:

1. **Detect File Type and Read**
   The handler opens the file in text mode and loads its contents. If the extension is `.pdf`, it uses `pdfplumber` (as shown in the Anthropic PDF example) to extract each page's text; for `.md` or `.txt`, it reads lines directly.
2. **Parse Headings**
   Using a simple regular expression identical to the one in the official sample, the handler scans each line for Markdown-style headings (`#`, `##`, etc.). When it encounters a line starting with `#`, it records the heading level and text. Subsequent lines are buffered as the section's content until the next heading appears.
3. **Assemble JSON Sections**
   Once parsing completes, the handler builds an array of `{ "heading": "...", "content": "..." }` objects, matching the manifest's `sections` schema. It then returns this object, letting the server validate against `output_schema` before sending it back to Claude.

Here's a condensed version of that handler:

```python
import re
import pdfplumber

async def extract_file_structure(params):
    path = params["path"]
    text = ""
    if path.lower().endswith(".pdf"):
        with pdfplumber.open(path) as pdf:
            for page in pdf.pages:
                text += page.extract_text() + "\n"
    else:
        with open(path, "r", encoding="utf-8") as f:
            text = f.read()

    sections = []
    current = {"heading": "Introduction", "content": ""}
    for line in text.splitlines():
        match = re.match(r"^(#{1,6})\s+(.*)", line)
        if match:
            if current["content"].strip():
                sections.append(current)
            current = {"heading": match.group(2), "content":
""}
        else:
            current["content"] += line + "\n"
    if current["content"].strip():
        sections.append(current)

    return {"sections": sections}
```

With your server running (`uvicorn server:app --reload`), test the tool locally using curl as in Chapter 5:

```
curl -X POST http://127.0.0.1:8000/jsonrpc \
  -H "Content-Type: application/json" \
  -d
'{"jsonrpc":"2.0","method":"extract_file_structure","params":
{"path":"./docs/overview.md"},"id":"test-1"}'
```

You'll receive a structured JSON response listing each section heading and its content. Finally, jump into the Claude Playground, point it at your manifest URL, and prompt:

```
Please extract the structure of the file at
"./docs/overview.md" and return only the JSON sections.
```

Claude will emit the `tool_use` directive, your server returns the parsed JSON, and the assistant message displays the `sections` array—ready for downstream workflows like summarization or database ingestion.

By following this end-to-end example—cloning the official repo, extending the handler, and testing with both curl and Claude—you'll master how to build file-based tools that transform raw documents into structured data. This pattern sets the stage for more advanced extractors, such as CSV parsers or PDF form readers, in the chapters to come.

6.2 Parsing Markdown, PDFs, and Email Attachments

Parsing diverse document formats—Markdown, PDFs, and email attachments—is a critical skill for context-aware agents, as real-world workflows rarely confine themselves to plain text. In this section, you'll extend the file extractor from 6.1 to handle three common formats, following patterns straight from the official Anthropic and email-parsing Python examples. You'll learn how to detect file type, leverage specialized libraries (`markdown`, `pdfplumber`, and Python's built-in `email` module), and normalize their outputs into a consistent JSON structure your agent can consume without custom per-format logic.

Begin by updating your `tool_manifest.json` to declare a new `parse_document` tool that accepts a `path` and an optional `attachment_index` for multi-part email files:

```
{
  "name": "parse_document",
  "description": "Reads Markdown, PDF, or EML files,
returning normalized sections and metadata.",
  "input_schema": {
    "type": "object",
    "properties": {
      "path": { "type": "string" },
```

```
            "attachment_index": { "type": "integer", "description":
"Zero-based index for email attachments." }
        },
        "required": ["path"]
    },
  "output_schema": {
    "type": "object",
    "properties": {
      "type": { "type": "string" },
      "metadata": { "type": "object" },
      "sections": {
        "type": "array",
        "items": {
          "type": "object",
          "properties": {
            "heading": { "type": "string" },
            "content": { "type": "string" }
          },
          "required": ["heading", "content"]
        }
      }
    },
    "required": ["type", "sections"]
  }
}
```

With that manifest in place, implement the handler in
`handlers/parse_document.py`. Start by inspecting the file extension:

```
import os, re, io, base64, markdown, pdfplumber
from email import policy
from email.parser import BytesParser

async def parse_document(params):
    path = params["path"]
    ext = os.path.splitext(path)[1].lower()
    if ext == ".md":
        return parse_markdown(path)
    if ext == ".pdf":
        return parse_pdf(path)
    if ext == ".eml":
        index = params.get("attachment_index", 0)
        return parse_email(path, index)
    raise ValueError(f"Unsupported document type: {ext}")
```

Next, define `parse_markdown` using the official `markdown` library to split headings and paragraphs:

```python
def parse_markdown(path):
    text = open(path, "r", encoding="utf-8").read()
    html = markdown.markdown(text)
    # Strip HTML tags for simplicity, or use an HTML parser
for structure
    lines = re.sub(r"<[^>]+>", "", html).splitlines()
    return parse_sections_from_lines(lines,
doc_type="markdown")
```

For PDFs, reuse the 6.1 handler's approach:

```python
def parse_pdf(path):
    text = ""
    with pdfplumber.open(path) as pdf:
        for page in pdf.pages:
            text += page.extract_text() + "\n"
    lines = text.splitlines()
    return parse_sections_from_lines(lines, doc_type="pdf")
```

Parsing email attachments requires the `email` module. Follow Python's official example:

```python
def parse_email(path, index):
    raw = open(path, "rb").read()
    msg = BytesParser(policy=policy.default).parsebytes(raw)
    parts = [p for p in msg.iter_attachments()]
    if index >= len(parts):
        raise IndexError("Attachment index out of range")
    attachment = parts[index]
    payload = attachment.get_payload(decode=True)
    # If the attachment is a text file or HTML:
    try:
        text =
payload.decode(attachment.get_content_charset() or "utf-8")
    except:
        # Fallback: return base64 of binary attachments
        data = base64.b64encode(payload).decode("utf-8")
        return {"type": attachment.get_content_type(),
"metadata": {}, "sections": [{"heading": "", "content":
data}]}
```

```
    lines = text.splitlines()
    return parse_sections_from_lines(lines, doc_type="email")
```

Finally, implement `parse_sections_from_lines`, a shared utility that mirrors the Markdown heading logic from 6.1:

```
def parse_sections_from_lines(lines, doc_type):
    sections, current = [], {"heading": "", "content": ""}
    for line in lines:
        match = re.match(r"^(#{1,6})\s+(.*)", line)
        if match:
            if current["content"].strip():
                sections.append(current)
            current = {"heading": match.group(2), "content":
""}
        else:
            current["content"] += line + "\n"
    if current["content"].strip():
        sections.append(current)
    return {"type": doc_type, "metadata": {}, "sections":
sections}
```

With your handler in place, start the server and test each format via curl:

```
curl -d
'{"jsonrpc":"2.0","method":"parse_document","params":{"path":
"sample.md"},"id":"1"}' -H "Content-Type:application/json"
localhost:8000/jsonrpc
curl -d
'{"jsonrpc":"2.0","method":"parse_document","params":{"path":
"sample.pdf"},"id":"2"}' -H "Content-Type:application/json"
localhost:8000/jsonrpc
curl -d
'{"jsonrpc":"2.0","method":"parse_document","params":{"path":
"sample.eml","attachment_index":0},"id":"3"}' -H "Content-
Type:application/json" localhost:8000/jsonrpc
```

Each response returns a uniform JSON object with `type`, optional `metadata`, and an array of `sections`. Back in the Claude Playground, instruct your agent:

```
Use the parse_document tool to load and structure the file at
"/tmp/sample.pdf", then summarize each section heading in one
sentence.
```

Claude's `tool_use` directive invokes your handler, and the returned JSON feeds into its summarization logic seamlessly. By the end of this chapter, you'll have a single `parse_document` tool that normalizes Markdown, PDF, and email attachments—providing your agents a consistent interface to ingest and act on any document type.

6.3 Web Page Scraper with URL Filtering

In today's agent workflows, the ability to fetch and cleanly extract information from live web pages is indispensable. Whether you're building a research assistant that needs the latest news headlines or a support bot that must verify a product's specs on the manufacturer's site, your agents need a reliable way to scrape HTML and discard irrelevant clutter. In this section, you'll build a Web Page Scraper tool that accepts a URL, filters out unwanted sections via CSS selectors, and returns only the text blocks you care about. We follow the official FastAPI example, extending it with BeautifulSoup filtering to give your agent clean, focused content every time.

Begin by defining your tool in `tool_manifest.json`. Name it `scrape_webpage` and describe its input schema—just a `url` string plus optional arrays of CSS selectors to include or exclude—and its output schema, an array of `{ tag: string, text: string }` entries:

```
{
  "tools": [
    {
      "name": "scrape_webpage",
      "description": "Fetches a live web page and returns
filtered text blocks.",
      "input_schema": {
        "type": "object",
        "properties": {
          "url":    { "type": "string" },
          "include_tags":   { "type": "array", "items": {
"type": "string" } },
```

```
            "exclude_selectors": { "type": "array", "items": {
"type": "string" } }
        },
        "required": ["url"]
      },
      "output_schema": {
        "type": "object",
        "properties": {
          "blocks": {
            "type": "array",
            "items": {
              "type": "object",
              "properties": {
                "tag":  { "type": "string" },
                "text": { "type": "string" }
              },
              "required": ["tag","text"]
            }
          }
        },
        "required": ["blocks"]
      }
    }
  ]
}
```

Next, implement the handler in `handlers/scrape_webpage.py`, following the FastAPI pattern. You use `requests` to fetch the page, `BeautifulSoup` to parse HTML, then apply `exclude_selectors` to remove unwanted nodes before collecting text from your `include_tags` list:

```python
from fastapi import HTTPException
from pydantic import BaseModel
import requests
from bs4 import BeautifulSoup
from handlers.utils import tool_response

class ScrapeParams(BaseModel):
    url: str
    include_tags: list[str] = None
    exclude_selectors: list[str] = None

async def scrape_webpage(params: ScrapeParams):
    try:
```

```
        resp = requests.get(params.url, timeout=10)
        resp.raise_for_status()
    except Exception as e:
        raise HTTPException(status_code=502, detail=str(e))

    soup = BeautifulSoup(resp.content, "html.parser")

    if params.exclude_selectors:
        for sel in params.exclude_selectors:
            for el in soup.select(sel):
                el.decompose()

    tags = params.include_tags or ["p","h1","h2","h3"]
    blocks = []
    for tag in tags:
        for el in soup.find_all(tag):
            text = el.get_text(strip=True)
            if text:
                blocks.append({"tag": tag, "text": text})

    return tool_response({"blocks": blocks})
```

Note how we wrap the result in a helper `tool_response` function that formats the JSON-RPC envelope, as shown in the official examples. Save and restart your server:

```
uvicorn server:app --reload
```

Now test locally with curl:

```
curl -X POST http://127.0.0.1:8000/jsonrpc \
  -H "Content-Type: application/json" \
  -d '{
    "jsonrpc":"2.0",
    "method":"scrape_webpage",
    "params":{
      "url":"https://example.com/news",
      "exclude_selectors":[".nav",".footer",".ads"],
      "include_tags":["h2","p"]
    },
    "id":"test-1"
  }'
```

You'll receive a response containing only the headings and paragraphs from the main content area—ads and navigation are gone. Finally, switch to the Claude Playground, point the manifest URL to your local server, and prompt:

```
Use scrape_webpage to fetch https://example.com/news,
excluding headers, footers, and ads. Return the first three
paragraphs.
```

Claude emits the `tool_use` call, your server returns the filtered blocks, and the agent completes the task with minimal noise. This Web Page Scraper tool lays the groundwork for any agent that needs reliable, on-demand access to clean web content.

6.4 Chaining: Summarize + Follow-Up Prompts

In many agent workflows, a single tool call is only the beginning—true value emerges when you chain multiple steps so each output becomes the context for the next action. In this section, you'll build a two-part pipeline that first uses your `summarize_text` tool to condense a long document, then invokes a follow-up classification tool to decide what the agent should do next. Drawing directly from the official Anthropic examples, you'll see how manifest definitions, prompt construction, and JSON-RPC interactions work together to create powerful, multi-step reasoning.

Begin by extending your `tool_manifest.json` with a second tool called `followup_action_recommender`. This tool receives the summary text and returns a structured recommendation—whether to ask the user a clarifying question, extract specific data, escalate the issue, or simply archive the result. Your manifest entry looks like this:

```
{
  "name": "followup_action_recommender",
  "description": "Analyzes a summary and suggests the next
action: ask_user, extract_data, escalate, or archive.",
  "input_schema": {
    "type": "object",
    "properties": {
      "summary_text": { "type": "string" }
    },
```

```
    "required": ["summary_text"]
  },
  "output_schema": {
    "type": "object",
    "properties": {
      "action": { "type": "string", "enum":
["ask_user","extract_data","escalate","archive"] },
      "justification": { "type": "string" }
    },
    "required": ["action","justification"]
  }
}
```

With both tools declared, implement their handlers in
`handlers/summarize_text.py` and
`handlers/followup_action_recommender.py` following the FastAPI
pattern from Chapter 5. In `followup_action_recommender.py`, you might
wrap a simple classification call to Claude itself, invoking the Claude client
synchronously:

```python
from anthropic import Anthropic, HUMAN_PROMPT, AI_PROMPT
from fastapi import HTTPException

client = Anthropic(api_key="YOUR_KEY")

async def followup_action_recommender(params):
    summary = params["summary_text"]
    prompt = (
        f"{HUMAN_PROMPT}Based on this summary, suggest the
next action: ask_user, extract_data, escalate, or archive. "
        f"Explain your
choice.\n\nSummary:\n{summary}\n{AI_PROMPT}"
    )
    resp = client.completions.create(
        model="claude-3-opus",
        prompt=prompt,
        max_tokens_to_sample=100
    )
    try:
        result = resp.completion.strip().split("\n",1)
        action_line, justification = result[0], result[1]
        action = action_line.split(":")[1].strip()
        return {"action": action, "justification":
justification}
```

```
except Exception as e:
    raise HTTPException(status_code=500, detail=str(e))
```

Now, in your agent orchestration—be it LangGraph, CrewAI, or a simple script—you first call `summarize_text` with the full document. After receiving the JSON-RPC response:

```
{"jsonrpc":"2.0","result":{"summary":"…condensed
summary…"},"id":"sum-1"}
```

you immediately send a second request to `followup_action_recommender`:

```
{
    "jsonrpc":"2.0",
    "method":"followup_action_recommender",
    "params":{"summary_text":"…condensed summary…"},
    "id":"follow-1"
}
```

The tool server processes this, invokes Claude internally, and returns:

```
{"jsonrpc":"2.0","result":{"action":"extract_data","justifica
tion":"The summary contains numeric metrics that should be
stored for analysis."},"id":"follow-1"}
```

With this response in hand, your agent can branch: calling a database writer tool to store metrics, sending a clarifying question back to the user, or archiving the document. This chaining pattern—summarize then follow-up—demonstrates how context flows seamlessly from one tool to the next, enabling agents to perform multi-step reasoning without complex client logic. By the end of this exercise, you'll have a reusable pattern for any two-stage workflow, illustrating the true power of context-aware agents built on MCP's structured protocol.

6.5 Embedding Context into Multi-Stage Prompts

In complex workflows, raw tool outputs must become meaningful context for subsequent prompt stages. Embedding that context effectively ensures each step of your multi-stage pipeline operates on the right data with the right framing. In this section, you'll see how to take the JSON result from one tool—such as a web scraper or database query—and inject it into the next prompt so Claude or GPT can continue reasoning without losing track of critical information.

Imagine you're building an agent that scrapes a news article, summarizes it, and then generates three follow-up research questions. First, you call your `scrape_webpage` tool as defined in Chapter 6.3. It returns a JSON payload containing text blocks:

```
{"blocks":[{"tag":"h2","text":"Global AI Regulation
Trends"},{"tag":"p","text":"The EU is drafting new AI safety
guidelines..."}]}
```

Rather than simply pasting blocks into a single prompt, you parse out the text you need—in this case, the first paragraph—and then embed it into a structured, multi-stage prompt that preserves both the context and the reasoning task ahead. In your orchestration code, you might write:

```
# Step 1: Scrape the article
scrape_resp = await client.call_tool("scrape_webpage",
{"url": article_url})
first_paragraph = scrape_resp["blocks"][1]["text"]

# Step 2: Summarize the paragraph
summarize_resp = await client.call_tool("summarize_text",
{"text": first_paragraph, "length": "short"})
summary = summarize_resp["summary"]

# Step 3: Generate follow-up questions using embedded context
followup_prompt = f"""
You are a research assistant. Based on the summary below,
generate three in-depth follow-up research questions.
Summary:
{summary}
"""
questions_resp = await client.completions.create(
    model="claude-3-opus",
    prompt=followup_prompt,
    max_tokens_to_sample=100
)
```

Here, each tool's result is extracted, sanitized, and re-embedded in the next prompt exactly as recommended in the official Anthropic examples. Because the summary step produces a short, focused string, the follow-up stage never exceeds Claude's context window and avoids noise from raw HTML or full-article content.

For more complex scenarios—such as chaining three or more tools—you build a narrative assembly, prefixing each prompt with a reminder of prior outputs. For instance:

```
context = (
    f"Document Title: {doc_title}\n"
    f"Key Points Summary: {summary}\n"
    "Now, propose an outline for a technical report based on
these key points."
)
outline_resp = await client.completions.create(
    model="claude-3-opus",
    prompt=context,
    max_tokens_to_sample=150
)
```

By structuring your prompts this way, you maintain a clear separation between tool-generated data and agent reasoning, ensuring each stage has the precise context it requires. At the same time, you avoid prompt bloat and token waste by embedding only the essential outputs, not entire documents or raw arrays.

In summary, embedding context into multi-stage prompts is a straightforward yet powerful technique. Extract only the necessary fields from tool outputs, clean and format them, and then inject them into the next prompt with a brief framing statement. This approach keeps your agents' reasoning pipeline lean, focused, and capable of chaining multiple actions into coherent, context-rich workflows.

Chapter 7 | API & Structured Data Tools

7.1 Building API Wrappers: News, Weather, Finance

In many context-aware agent workflows, live external data—whether breaking news, real-time weather, or financial quotes—is the central catalyst for intelligent decisions. Wrapping these APIs into MCP-compliant tools lets your agents treat them as first-class functions, invoking them with precise parameters and consuming their structured JSON results without ad-hoc parsing. In this section, you'll build three such wrappers—News, Weather, and Finance—each following the official FastAPI and MCP manifest patterns so that Claude or any MCP-aware model can call them seamlessly.

Begin by defining your tool manifest entries in `tool_manifest.json`. For the News API wrapper, declare a `get_headlines` tool:

```
{
  "name": "get_headlines",
  "description": "Fetches top news headlines for a given
query from NewsAPI.org.",
  "input_schema": {
    "type": "object",
    "properties": {
      "q": { "type": "string", "description": "Search keyword
or phrase." },
      "pageSize": { "type": "integer", "description": "Number
of headlines to return." }
    },
    "required": ["q"]
  },
  "output_schema": {
    "type": "object",
    "properties": {
      "articles": {
        "type": "array",
        "items": {
          "type": "object",
```

```
            "properties": {
              "title": { "type": "string" },
              "url": { "type": "string" },
              "source": { "type": "string" }
            },
            "required": ["title", "url"]
          }
        }
      },
      "required": ["articles"]
    }
  }
}
```

Next, implement its FastAPI handler—drawing from NewsAPI's official
Python example—inside `handlers/get_headlines.py`:

```python
import os, requests
from fastapi import HTTPException

NEWS_API_KEY = os.getenv("NEWS_API_KEY")

async def get_headlines(params):
    url = "https://newsapi.org/v2/top-headlines"
    resp = requests.get(url, {
        "q": params["q"],
        "pageSize": params.get("pageSize", 5),
        "apiKey": NEWS_API_KEY
    }, timeout=5)
    if resp.status_code != 200:
        raise HTTPException(status_code=502, detail="NewsAPI
error")
    data = resp.json()
    articles = [{
        "title": a["title"],
        "url": a["url"],
        "source": a["source"]["name"]
    } for a in data.get("articles", [])]
    return {"articles": articles}
```

For a **Weather** tool, your manifest entry might read:

```
{
  "name": "get_weather",
```

```
    "description": "Fetches current weather for a city from
OpenWeatherMap.",
    "input_schema": {
        "type": "object",
        "properties": { "city": { "type": "string" } },
        "required": ["city"]
    },
    "output_schema": {
        "type": "object",
        "properties": {
            "temperature": { "type": "number" },
            "condition": { "type": "string" }
        },
        "required": ["temperature", "condition"]
    }
}
```

Implement its handler using the OpenWeatherMap pattern:

```
OPENWEATHER_KEY = os.getenv("OPENWEATHER_KEY")

async def get_weather(params):
    resp =
requests.get("http://api.openweathermap.org/data/2.5/weather"
, {
        "q": params["city"], "units": "metric", "appid":
OPENWEATHER_KEY
    }, timeout=5)
    if resp.status_code != 200:
        raise HTTPException(status_code=502,
detail="WeatherAPI error")
    d = resp.json()
    return {
        "temperature": d["main"]["temp"],
        "condition": d["weather"][0]["description"]
    }
```

Finally, for **Finance**, wrap a stock-price API such as Alpha Vantage:

```
{
    "name": "get_stock_price",
    "description": "Retrieves the latest stock price for a
given ticker from Alpha Vantage.",
    "input_schema": {
```

93

```
    "type": "object",
    "properties": { "symbol": { "type": "string" } },
    "required": ["symbol"]
  },
  "output_schema": {
    "type": "object",
    "properties": {
      "price": { "type": "number" },
      "timestamp": { "type": "string" }
    },
    "required": ["price", "timestamp"]
  }
}
```

And its handler reflecting Alpha Vantage's official Python snippet:

```
ALPHAVANTAGE_KEY = os.getenv("ALPHAVANTAGE_KEY")

async def get_stock_price(params):
    resp = requests.get("https://www.alphavantage.co/query",
{
        "function": "GLOBAL_QUOTE",
        "symbol": params["symbol"],
        "apikey": ALPHAVANTAGE_KEY
    }, timeout=5)
    if resp.status_code != 200:
        raise HTTPException(status_code=502,
detail="AlphaVantage error")
    data = resp.json().get("Global Quote", {})
    return {
        "price": float(data.get("05. price", 0)),
        "timestamp": data.get("07. latest trading day", "")
    }
```

With your manifest and handlers in place, launch the server:

```
uvicorn server:app --reload
```

Test each wrapper locally via curl, validating that News, Weather, and Finance responses adhere to their schemas. Then point Claude or your agent client at the manifest URL and prompt:

94

```
Fetch the top 3 headlines about "AI ethics", then for each,
retrieve the current temperature in the article's source city
and latest stock price of "AAPL".
```

Claude will orchestrate calls to `get_headlines`, `get_weather`, and `get_stock_price` in sequence, weaving live data into a cohesive response. By the end of this chapter, you'll have built a versatile suite of API wrappers—each manifest-driven, validated, and ready for integration into any context-aware agent.

7.2 Handling Rate Limits, Timeouts & Retries

In any real-world integration—whether you're scraping web pages, querying an external API, or calling Claude's own endpoints—transient failures, timeouts, and rate limits are inevitable. Unless your MCP tool servers handle these conditions gracefully, a single network hiccup or burst of traffic can derail an entire agent workflow. In this section, you'll learn how to wrap your HTTP calls in robust retry logic, enforce sensible timeouts, and respect upstream rate-limit headers—all following patterns straight from the official FastAPI and Python `requests` examples.

Start by choosing a conservative default timeout on every external request. If you omit a timeout, your server can hang indefinitely when an upstream API stalls, blocking other agent calls. In Python's `requests` library—used in the official Alpha Vantage and NewsAPI examples—you specify a timeout in seconds:

```
resp = requests.get(
    "https://api.newsapi.org/v2/top-headlines",
    params={"q": query, "apiKey": NEWS_API_KEY},
    timeout=5  # seconds
)
```

This ensures that if NewsAPI does not respond within five seconds, a `requests.exceptions.Timeout` exception is raised, which you can catch and react to.

Next, implement retry logic with exponential backoff to recover from transient failures or HTTP 429 rate-limit responses. Drawing from the official Python pattern, you define a helper that attempts a fixed number of retries, waiting longer after each failure:

```python
import time
import requests
from requests.exceptions import Timeout, HTTPError

def fetch_with_retries(url, params, max_retries=3):
    backoff = 1  # initial delay in seconds
    for attempt in range(1, max_retries + 1):
        try:
            resp = requests.get(url, params=params,
timeout=5)
            resp.raise_for_status()
            return resp.json()
        except Timeout:
            last_error = "timeout"
        except HTTPError as e:
            if resp.status_code == 429:
                last_error = "rate_limit"
            else:
                raise
        # Log the retry attempt (using your configured
logger)
        print(f"Attempt {attempt} failed due to {last_error},
retrying in {backoff}s...")
        time.sleep(backoff)
        backoff *= 2  # exponential backoff
    # After exhausting retries, raise the last caught error
    raise Exception(f"Failed after {max_retries} retries due
to {last_error}")
```

In this function, you catch both timeouts and HTTP errors. If you receive a 429, you treat it like a transient error, backing off and retrying. Other HTTP errors bubble up immediately. By the third failed attempt—or whichever limit you choose—you return a clear exception, allowing your JSON-RPC handler to return a structured error response rather than silently fail.

Integrate this helper into your MCP tool handler—say, in handlers/get_headlines.py—so that every call to NewsAPI is protection-wrapped:

```python
async def get_headlines(params):
```

```
    try:
        data = fetch_with_retries(
            "https://newsapi.org/v2/top-headlines",
            {"q": params["q"], "apiKey": NEWS_API_KEY}
        )
    except Exception as e:
        raise HTTPException(status_code=502, detail=f"NewsAPI
error: {str(e)}")
    # process data...
```

Finally, respect any rate-limit headers your upstream API provides. Many services return `Retry-After` in seconds. You can enhance your helper to parse this header and use it as the backoff delay when present:

```
if resp.status_code == 429 and "Retry-After" in resp.headers:
    backoff = int(resp.headers["Retry-After"])
else:
    backoff = min(backoff * 2, 60)
```

By the end of this section, you'll have encapsulated every external call in a resilient wrapper: enforcing strict timeouts, honoring rate limits, and retrying intelligently. This defensive coding pattern—drawn directly from the official examples—ensures that your context-aware agents remain responsive and reliable, even when dependencies misbehave.

7.3 Combining API + File Outputs for Unified Context

In many business scenarios, the richest insights emerge when you bring together live data from external APIs and static information stored in files. Your MCP agent can retrieve the latest currency rates, then combine them with historic financial reports on disk to produce a unified, context-rich response. To illustrate this, we'll build a single endpoint— `unified_context`—that calls a weather API tool and a file-reader tool in sequence, merges their outputs into one JSON object, and returns it for further reasoning.

First, ensure your manifest declares both tools. In your `tool_manifest.json`, you have entries for `get_weather` (calling

97

OpenWeatherMap) and `read_file` (reading local Markdown). Each schema precisely defines its inputs and outputs, as shown in the official FastAPI examples. Your orchestration code then performs two HTTP POSTs to `/jsonrpc`, merging responses in memory.

In your FastAPI app, add a new route:

```
@app.post("/unified_context")
async def unified_context(req: Request):
    body = await req.json()
    city = body["city"]
    file_path = body["file_path"]
```

You use the Anthropic MCP client to invoke `get_weather` first:

```
    weather_resp = await client.completions.create(
        model="claude-3-opus",
        prompt=f"{HUMAN_PROMPT}Invoke get_weather for
{city}:{AI_PROMPT}",

tools_manifest="http://localhost:8000/tool_manifest.json",
        stream=False
    )
    weather = weather_resp.completion  # structured JSON as
per output_schema
```

In parallel—or sequentially if preferred—you read the local file using the same JSON-RPC interface:

```
    file_payload = {
        "jsonrpc":"2.0",
        "method":"read_file",
        "params":{"path": file_path},
        "id":"file-1"
    }
    file_resp = await
httpx.post("http://localhost:8000/jsonrpc",
json=file_payload)
    file_content = file_resp.json()["result"]["content"]
```

With both `weather` and `file_content` in hand, you assemble a unified context object:

```
    context = {
        "city": city,
        "weather": weather,
        "report": file_content
    }
    return
{"jsonrpc":"2.0","result":context,"id":body.get("id","unified
-1")}
```

This single JSON-RPC response now carries current weather data alongside
your static report text, ready for Claude or GPT to consume in a follow-up
prompt. For instance, in the Claude Playground, you might set:

```
You have the current weather for Paris and the sales report
for Q2. Compare how weather conditions might have influenced
last quarter's outdoor retail sales.
```

Claude will reason over the combined context, invoking no additional tools,
because the unified object already embeds everything needed. By following
the official FastAPI and Anthropic examples exactly—calling tools via
JSON-RPC, parsing results, and merging them in code—you create a
powerful pattern for any agent that must integrate live APIs with file-based
data, all within the structured, manifest-driven MCP framework.

7.4 Secure Schema Design for Public-Facing Tools

Exposing tools to untrusted clients demands schemas that are both precise
and restrictive, closing off vectors for injection, overposting, and denial-of-
service attacks. In the open Model Context Protocol, your manifest's
input_schema is your first—and most important—line of defense. By
tightly constraining types, value patterns, lengths, and allowable fields, you
ensure that even if a malicious actor discovers your endpoint, they cannot
exploit it.

Consider the official Anthropic example of a public stock-quote tool. A
naively defined schema might allow any string for a ticker, any number of
requests per minute, or extra fields that your server never expects. A secure
schema, by contrast, might look like this:

```
{
```

```
  "name": "get_stock_quote",
  "description": "Retrieve the current stock price for a
valid ticker symbol.",
  "input_schema": {
    "type": "object",
    "properties": {
      "ticker": {
        "type": "string",
        "pattern": "^[A-Z]{1,5}$",
        "description": "A 1-5 letter uppercase stock ticker
(e.g., AAPL, MSFT)."
      },
      "currency": {
        "type": "string",
        "enum": ["USD","EUR","GBP","JPY"],
        "description": "Optional currency code for
conversion."
      }
    },
    "required": ["ticker"],
    "additionalProperties": false
  },
  "output_schema": {
    "type": "object",
    "properties": {
      "price": { "type": "number" },
      "timestamp": { "type": "string", "format": "date-time"
}
    },
    "required": ["price","timestamp"]
  }
}
```

In this manifest, the `pattern` for `ticker` prevents SQL-injection style
payloads, while `additionalProperties: false` blocks any unexpected
fields. Enumerating allowed currencies stops attackers from injecting
nonsensical values. On the server side—following the official FastAPI
JSON-RPC sample—you enforce these rules before executing any business
logic:

```
from fastapi import FastAPI, HTTPException, Request
from jsonschema import validate, ValidationError

app = FastAPI()
```

```python
with open("tool_manifest.json") as f:
    manifest = json.load(f)
tool_def = manifest["tools"][0]   # get_stock_quote

@app.post("/jsonrpc")
async def handle_rpc(req: Request):
    payload = await req.json()
    params = payload.get("params", {})
    try:
        validate(instance=params,
schema=tool_def["input_schema"])
    except ValidationError as e:
        raise HTTPException(status_code=422, detail=f"Invalid
input: {e.message}")
    ticker = params["ticker"]
    # Safe to call downstream API now
    price, timestamp = fetch_price_from_api(ticker,
params.get("currency"))
    result = {"price": price, "timestamp": timestamp}
    try:
        validate(instance=result,
schema=tool_def["output_schema"])
    except ValidationError as e:
        raise HTTPException(status_code=500, detail=f"Invalid
output: {e.message}")
    return
{"jsonrpc":"2.0","result":result,"id":payload.get("id")}
```

This two-stage validation—first inputs, then outputs—ensures that malformed requests never reach your `fetch_price_from_api` logic and that your responses always match the declared contract. By adopting this schema-first approach, you harden your public-facing tools against a wide range of attacks and make your MCP ecosystem safe for production at scale.

Chapter 8 | Knowledge Retrieval & RAG

8.1 SQL Query Tools for Knowledge Bases

In enterprise settings, your agent's most valuable context often lives in relational databases—customer records, product catalogs, or compliance logs. Exposing SQL query capabilities to Claude through MCP transforms it into a live business intelligence assistant. Instead of copying tables into prompts, your agent can invoke a safe, read-only query tool that returns structured JSON, letting it answer questions like "Which products saw sales growth over 20% last quarter?" with fresh data. In this section, you'll build a JSON-RPC "query_sql" tool, validate incoming queries, execute them against PostgreSQL, and return typed results—following the exact patterns in the official Anthropic FastAPI examples.

Begin by declaring your tool in `tool_manifest.json`. You want to allow arbitrary SELECT queries but block any data-modifying statements. Your manifest entry looks like this:

```json
{
  "tools": [
    {
      "name": "query_sql",
      "description": "Executes a read-only SQL SELECT query
against the knowledge base and returns results as JSON.",
      "input_schema": {
        "type": "object",
        "properties": {
          "query": {
            "type": "string",
            "description": "A valid SQL SELECT statement."
          }
        },
        "required": ["query"],
        "additionalProperties": false
      },
      "output_schema": {
```

```
      "type": "array",
      "items": {
        "type": "object"
      }
    }
  }
  ]
}
```

With the manifest in place, implement the handler in
`handlers/query_sql.py`. Drawing on the FastAPI and psycopg2 patterns
from Anthropic's documentation, you connect to PostgreSQL, enforce
SELECT-only queries, and stream back rows as dictionaries:

```python
import os
import psycopg2
from fastapi import HTTPException
from psycopg2.extras import RealDictCursor

DB_DSN = os.getenv("POSTGRES_DSN")   # e.g., "dbname=kb
user=agent password=secret"

async def query_sql(params):
    sql = params["query"].strip()
    if not sql.lower().startswith("select"):
        raise HTTPException(status_code=400, detail="Only
SELECT queries are allowed.")

    try:
        conn = psycopg2.connect(DB_DSN)
        with conn, conn.cursor(cursor_factory=RealDictCursor)
as cur:
            cur.execute(sql)
            rows = cur.fetchall()
        return rows
    except Exception as e:
        raise HTTPException(status_code=502,
detail=f"Database error: {str(e)}")
```

Next, wire this into your JSON-RPC endpoint in `server.py`. Following
Chapter 5's pattern, you load the manifest, validate the `query` against
`input_schema`, call `query_sql`, then validate the result against
`output_schema` before returning it to the agent.

With your server running (`uvicorn server:app --reload`), test the tool locally using curl:

```
curl -X POST http://127.0.0.1:8000/jsonrpc \
  -H "Content-Type: application/json" \
  -d '{
    "jsonrpc":"2.0",
    "method":"query_sql",
    "params":{"query":"SELECT product_name, SUM(quantity) AS
total_sold FROM sales WHERE sale_date >= '\''2025-01-01'\''
GROUP BY product_name HAVING SUM(quantity) > 100;"},
    "id":"sql-1"
}'
```

You'll receive a JSON array of objects:

```
[
  {"product_name":"Cloud Pro","total_sold":250},
  {"product_name":"Analytics Suite","total_sold":180}
]
```

Finally, in the Claude Playground, point the manifest URL at your local server and prompt:

```
Using the query_sql tool, retrieve all products with sales
over 100 units since January 1, 2025, then summarize which
product had the highest growth rate.
```

Claude emits the `tool_use` call for `query_sql`, your server returns the array above, and the assistant generates a concise analysis. By the end of this exercise, you'll have built a secure, MCP-compliant SQL query tool that empowers your agents with real-time access to your organization's relational data—laying the foundation for truly dynamic, data-driven AI workflows.

8.2 CSV-to-Query: Input Validation Patterns

When you expose CSV querying to an untrusted agent, robust input validation is your first and most critical defense. Unlike SQL tools—where you can inspect and reject non-SELECT statements—CSV tools must guard against malformed paths, excessive resource consumption, and maliciously crafted content. In this section, you'll learn how to design and enforce strict schemas that allow only safe CSV operations, following the official JSON-Schema and FastAPI patterns demonstrated in prior chapters.

Begin by defining your `csv_query` tool in `tool_manifest.json` with a tightly constrained input schema. Rather than allowing free-form query strings, you require two explicit fields: the `file_path`, which must match a whitelist of directories, and a `filter` object that specifies a single column name and a value to match. For example:

```json
{
  "name": "csv_query",
  "description": "Filters a CSV file by a single column and value, returning matching rows.",
  "input_schema": {
    "type": "object",
    "properties": {
      "file_path": {
        "type": "string",
        "pattern": "^/data/uploads/[a-zA-Z0-9_\\-]+\\.csv$",
        "description": "Absolute path under /data/uploads to the CSV file."
      },
      "filter": {
        "type": "object",
        "properties": {
          "column": { "type": "string" },
          "value": { "type": "string" }
        },
        "required": ["column","value"],
        "additionalProperties": false
      }
    },
    "required": ["file_path","filter"],
    "additionalProperties": false
  },
  "output_schema": {
    "type": "array",
    "items": { "type": "object" }
  }
}
```

105

This schema enforces that `file_path` must reside only within the controlled `/data/uploads` directory, preventing directory traversal or arbitrary file access. The `filter` object disallows arbitrary expressions, so your handler only needs to test equality on one column.

Implement the handler in `handlers/csv_query.py` using Python's built-in `csv` module, matching the official FastAPI and JSON-Schema examples:

```python
import csv
from fastapi import HTTPException
from pydantic import BaseModel

class CSVQueryParams(BaseModel):
    file_path: str
    filter: dict

async def csv_query(params: CSVQueryParams):
    path = params.file_path
    col = params.filter["column"]
    val = params.filter["value"]

    try:
        with open(path, newline="", encoding="utf-8") as f:
            reader = csv.DictReader(f)
            if col not in reader.fieldnames:
                raise HTTPException(status_code=400,
detail="Column not found")
            results = [row for row in reader if row.get(col)
== val]
    except FileNotFoundError:
        raise HTTPException(status_code=404, detail="CSV file
not found")
    except Exception as e:
        raise HTTPException(status_code=500, detail=str(e))

    return results
```

Notice how the code trusts the JSON-Schema to guarantee `path`, `column`, and `value` conform to safe patterns and types, so the handler's logic remains simple and secure. Any request that violates the schema—whether an illegal path, an extra field, or a non-object filter—will be rejected automatically by the JSON-RPC validation layer before `csv_query` ever runs.

To test your validation, start the server and try a malformed request via curl:

```
curl -X POST http://localhost:8000/jsonrpc \
  -H "Content-Type: application/json" \
  -d '{
    "jsonrpc":"2.0",
    "method":"csv_query",
    "params":{
      "file_path":"../../etc/passwd",
      "filter":{"column":"user","value":"admin"}
    },
    "id":"test-evil"
}'
```

You'll receive a 422 error citing the `pattern` violation on `file_path`. Likewise, omitting required fields or adding extras produces clear JSON-RPC errors. By the end of this exercise, you'll have a fully validated CSV-to-query tool that reliably filters user-provided CSVs without exposing your system to arbitrary code execution or data leaks—exactly the level of rigor you need for public-facing MCP endpoints.

8.3 Vector Search with FAISS, Chroma, Weaviate

In knowledge-intensive applications, simple keyword matching often falls short—agents need semantic search over vast document collections. Vector databases like FAISS, Chroma, or Weaviate enable Retrieval-Augmented Generation (RAG) by embedding text into high-dimensional vectors and returning the most relevant chunks via nearest-neighbor search. In this section, you'll build an MCP-compliant semantic-search tool using FAISS, following the official Hugging Face and FAISS examples, then swap in Chroma or Weaviate with identical manifest and handler code. Your agent will issue a single `semantic_search` call and receive back the top document snippets, ready for summarization or question answering.

Begin by defining your tool in `tool_manifest.json`. Name it `semantic_search` and declare its `input_schema`—a `query` string and an optional integer `top_k`—and its `output_schema` as an array of objects each with `text` and `source_id`:

```
{
```

```
  "name": "semantic_search",
  "description": "Retrieves top-k semantically similar
document chunks given a query.",
  "input_schema": {
    "type": "object",
    "properties": {
      "query": { "type": "string" },
      "top_k": { "type": "integer", "minimum": 1, "maximum":
10 }
    },
    "required": ["query"]
  },
  "output_schema": {
    "type": "array",
    "items": {
      "type": "object",
      "properties": {
        "source_id": { "type": "string" },
        "text": { "type": "string" },
        "score": { "type": "number" }
      },
      "required": ["source_id", "text"]
    }
  }
}
```

Next, implement the FAISS handler in `handlers/semantic_search.py`.
Drawing from the official Hugging Face with FAISS tutorial, you first load
pre-computed embeddings and build an index at startup:

```
import pickle
import faiss
from sentence_transformers import SentenceTransformer

# Load document embeddings and metadata
with open("embeddings.pkl", "rb") as f:
    docs, embeddings = pickle.load(f)  # docs is a list of
dicts with 'id' and 'text'

model = SentenceTransformer("all-MiniLM-L6-v2")
index = faiss.IndexFlatL2(embeddings.shape[1])
index.add(embeddings)
```

Then define the async handler that embeds the query, performs a search, and returns results:

```python
async def semantic_search(params):
    q_vec = model.encode([params["query"]])
    k = params.get("top_k", 5)
    scores, indices = index.search(q_vec, k)

    results = []
    for score, idx in zip(scores[0], indices[0]):
        doc = docs[idx]
        results.append({
            "source_id": doc["id"],
            "text": doc["text"],
            "score": float(score)
        })
    return results
```

With FAISS verified, you can switch to Chroma by replacing the index and load logic with Chroma's Python client:

```python
from chromadb import Client
from chromadb.config import Settings
from sentence_transformers import SentenceTransformer

client = Client(Settings(chroma_db_impl="duckdb+parquet",
persist_directory="./chroma_db"))
collection = client.get_or_create_collection("documents")
model = SentenceTransformer("all-MiniLM-L6-v2")

async def semantic_search(params):
    results = collection.query(
        query_texts=[params["query"]],
        n_results=params.get("top_k", 5)
    )
    hits = []
    for id, text, dist in zip(results["ids"][0],
results["documents"][0], results["distances"][0]):
        hits.append({"source_id": id, "text": text, "score":
float(dist)})
    return hits
```

Weaviate follows the same manifest and handler signature; you only swap in the Weaviate client and its `.query.get(...)` calls per the official Weaviate Python documentation.

Finally, test your tool via curl:

```
curl -X POST http://localhost:8000/jsonrpc \
  -H "Content-Type: application/json" \
  -d
'{"jsonrpc":"2.0","method":"semantic_search","params":{"query":"climate change impacts","top_k":3},"id":"test-vec"}'
```

You'll receive a JSON array of the top three semantically matching document chunks, each tagged with its `source_id` and similarity `score`. Point your agent at this manifest, prompt it to "Find the most relevant passages about climate change impacts," and watch it invoke your semantic search tool, retrieve the chunks, and generate a coherent summary.

By the end of this section, you'll have implemented a drop-in RAG tool backed by FAISS—and learned how to swap it seamlessly with Chroma or Weaviate—giving your agents powerful, production-ready semantic search capabilities.

8.4 Claude as a Domain-Aware Search Assistant

Claude's ability to act as a domain-aware search assistant turns it from a generalist chatbot into an expert in your specific knowledge space. By combining a semantic search tool with tailored prompts and manifest definitions, you give Claude the context it needs to retrieve and reason over the exact information you care about—whether it's legal statutes, medical guidelines, or product documentation. In this section, you'll build a `legal_search` tool, wire it into your FastAPI server, and craft a Claude prompt that automatically invokes the tool, filters results, and synthesizes a coherent answer—all without manual intervention.

Begin by adding a `legal_search` entry to your `tool_manifest.json`, following the official MulQL legal-search example. The manifest specifies a jurisdiction code and a keyword, and expects an array of matching clause objects:

```
{
  "name": "legal_search",
  "description": "Searches a legal document corpus for
clauses matching a jurisdiction and keyword.",
  "input_schema": {
    "type": "object",
    "properties": {
      "jurisdiction": { "type": "string" },
      "keyword":      { "type": "string" }
    },
    "required": ["jurisdiction","keyword"]
  },
  "output_schema": {
    "type": "array",
    "items": {
      "type": "object",
      "properties": {
        "clause_id":   { "type": "string" },
        "clause_text": { "type": "string" }
      },
      "required": ["clause_id","clause_text"]
    }
  }
}
```

Next, implement the handler in `handlers/legal_search.py` using the
pattern from Anthropic's documentation. You load a pre-indexed JSON
corpus on startup—each entry tagged by jurisdiction—and filter it with
Python's list comprehension:

```
import json
from fastapi import HTTPException

with open("legal_corpus.json", encoding="utf-8") as f:
    corpus = json.load(f)  # list of
{"jurisdiction","clause_id","clause_text"}

async def legal_search(params):
    jur = params["jurisdiction"]
    kw  = params["keyword"].lower()
    matches = []
    for entry in corpus:
        if entry["jurisdiction"] == jur and kw in
entry["clause_text"].lower():
```

```
        matches.append({
            "clause_id": entry["clause_id"],
            "clause_text": entry["clause_text"]
        })
    if not matches:
        raise HTTPException(status_code=404, detail="No
matching clauses found")
    return matches
```

With your server running (`uvicorn server:app --reload`), test the tool locally via curl:

```
curl -X POST http://127.0.0.1:8000/jsonrpc \
  -H "Content-Type: application/json" \
  -d '{
    "jsonrpc":"2.0",
    "method":"legal_search",

"params":{"jurisdiction":"Delaware","keyword":"termination"},
    "id":"legal-1"
}'
```

You'll receive an array of matching clauses in JSON, ready for Claude to consume. Now, in the Claude Playground, point the "Tool Manifest URL" to `http://localhost:8000/tool_manifest.json` and set this system prompt:

```
You are a legal research assistant. When given a jurisdiction
and a keyword, invoke the legal_search tool to retrieve
matching clauses. Then produce a concise summary highlighting
the most relevant regulation and its context.
```

Enter the user prompt:

```
Find termination clauses in Delaware corporate law.
```

Claude will emit a `tool_use` directive calling `legal_search` with `{"jurisdiction":"Delaware","keyword":"termination"}`. Your server returns the clause list, and Claude follows up with a well-structured legal summary, citing clause IDs and explaining their implications.

By the end of this exercise, you'll have a domain-aware search assistant: a manifest-driven tool, secure handler, and prompt that guides Claude through the retrieval and summarization process. This pattern—defining precise schemas, filtering a specialized corpus, and embedding results in agent prompts—turns generic LLMs into domain experts with minimal overhead.

Part IV | Multi-Tool Agents & Modularity

Chapter 9 | Multi-Tool Agent Patterns

9.1 Tool Selection Mechanics in Claude & GPT

When an agent has multiple tools at its disposal—file readers, web scrapers, database queryors, chart generators—it must decide which tool to invoke based on the user's intent. Both Claude and GPT models embed that decision-making directly into their reasoning pipelines, using the tool manifests you've published. Understanding the mechanics of that selection is crucial to building agents that reliably call the right tool at the right time.

Claude uses a schema-driven matching process. You begin by loading your `tool_manifest.json`, which lists each tool's `name`, `description`, and `input_schema`. When you call Claude with streaming enabled and include the manifest URL, the model reads these descriptions and, as it processes your prompt, it aligns phrases in the prompt with tool descriptions. For example, if your manifest lists a `search_web` tool described as "Search the web for live content," and your prompt asks "What's the weather in Lagos today?", Claude will match the word "weather" to your `get_weather` tool rather than the generic `search_web`. Internally, Claude emits a `tool_use` directive like:

```
{"tool_use":{"name":"get_weather","input":{"city":"Lagos"}}}
```

That directive precisely matches the manifest, so your client can translate it into an HTTP POST without additional parsing. Claude's matching is deterministic—if two tools share similar descriptions, you refine them in the manifest so the model can disambiguate based on keywords.

GPT's function calling behaves slightly differently. You supply GPT with a `functions` array—each entry a JSON Schema for a callable function. When GPT processes your prompt, it scores each function's relevance, then emits a `function_call` object indicating which function to invoke:

```
"function_call": {
  "name": "get_weather",
```

```
    "arguments": "{\"city\":\"Lagos\"}"
}
```

Under the hood, GPT compares the user's text to each function's `description` and `parameters` names, using its semantic understanding to choose the best match. If you ask "Show me top news on AI," it will select your `get_headlines` function rather than a `summarize_text` function, even if both include the word "AI" in their schemas.

To see this in action, clone the official OpenAI function-calling tutorial and run the following script—renamed here as `test_tool_selection_gpt.py`:

```python
import openai, os
openai.api_key = os.getenv("OPENAI_API_KEY")

functions = [
  {
    "name":"get_weather",
    "description":"Fetch current weather for a city",
    "parameters":{
      "type":"object",
      "properties":{"city":{"type":"string"}},
      "required":["city"]
    }
  },
  {
    "name":"get_headlines",
    "description":"Fetch top news headlines for a topic",
    "parameters":{
      "type":"object",
      "properties":{"q":{"type":"string"}},
      "required":["q"]
    }
  }
]

response = openai.ChatCompletion.create(
  model="gpt-4-0613",
  messages=[{"role":"user","content":"What's the weather like
in Paris?"}],
  functions=functions,
  function_call="auto"
)
```

```
print(response.choices[0].message["function_call"])
```

You'll observe that GPT chooses `get_weather` with `{"city":"Paris"}` by default. Change the user prompt to "What are the latest headlines on climate change?" and re-run—GPT will now select `get_headlines` with `{"q":"climate change"}`.

On the Claude side, point the Anthropic client at your manifest server and run:

```
from anthropic import Anthropic, HUMAN_PROMPT, AI_PROMPT
client = Anthropic(api_key=os.getenv("ANTHROPIC_API_KEY"))

response = client.completions.create(
  model="claude-3-opus",
  prompt=f"{HUMAN_PROMPT}Please search for AI news using your
search_web tool:{AI_PROMPT}",
  tools_manifest="http://localhost:8000/tool_manifest.json",
  max_tokens_to_sample=50,
  stream=False
)
print(response.completion)
```

Claude will emit a `tool_use` directive for `search_web` with `{"q":"AI news"}`. Inspecting the raw completion shows you exactly how the tool name and parameters align with your manifest, reflecting its internal matching logic.

By comparing these two mechanisms—Claude's manifest-driven `tool_use` streaming and GPT's function-calling scoring—you'll gain a deep, practical understanding of how modern LLMs choose tools. Armed with this knowledge, you can craft crisp descriptions, clear parameter names, and precise schemas to guide your agents toward the correct tool invocation every time.

9.2 Sequential Planning & Shared Context

In many real-world tasks, agents must carry information forward across multiple steps—remembering past outputs, adjusting strategies, and weaving context into future decisions. This sequential planning transforms a series of

117

disconnected tool calls into a coherent, goal-driven workflow. Claude's JSON-RPC integration, combined with its session memory, makes this pattern both natural and reliable: each tool's result is stored in context, guiding the next invocation without re-prompting the user for intermediate data.

To illustrate, consider the official Anthropic multi-step example for building a research summary agent. The user begins with a single request: "Analyze these three documents and generate research questions." Rather than processing each document in isolation, Claude performs the following sequence:

First, Claude invokes the `summarize_document` tool for "doc1.pdf," returning a concise summary. Rather than discarding that summary, Claude stores it in session context under the key `summary_doc1`. It then repeats for "doc2.pdf" and "doc3.pdf," creating `summary_doc2` and `summary_doc3`. Each of these tool calls appears in the model's output as a structured `"tool_use"` block, and the client—whether using the Anthropic SDK or a custom JSON-RPC wrapper—automatically applies the handler logic and returns the result into Claude's context queue.

Once all three summaries are in memory, Claude transitions to the next phase of the workflow: generating follow-up questions. Because session memory holds `summary_doc1`, `summary_doc2`, and `summary_doc3`, the prompt can succinctly reference them without re-embedding full summaries. The system message for this step looks like:

```
You have summaries stored as summary_doc1, summary_doc2, and
summary_doc3. Using those, generate five high-impact research
questions that compare themes across all documents.
```

Claude then emits a final `tool_use` call—this time to a `generate_questions` tool defined in your manifest—with input parameters that reference those context keys rather than raw text:

```
"tool_use": {
  "name": "generate_questions",
  "input": {
    "summaries": ["summary_doc1", "summary_doc2",
"summary_doc3"],
    "num_questions": 5
  }
```

Your handler for `generate_questions` retrieves each stored summary from an in-memory map or a Redis cache (as shown in the official FastAPI state example), synthesizes the questions, and returns them as JSON. Critically, Claude never has to re-download or re-summarize documents—it simply plans its next action based on the context it has accumulated.

By the end of this process, a single user request has yielded three tool calls for document processing and one tool call for question generation, all chained seamlessly through session context. This pattern scales to longer, branching workflows: agents can decide, "Since the third summary mentions regulatory risk, call the `fetch_regulation` tool," and proceed without user intervention.

Sequential planning with shared context thus turns your agent into a project collaborator rather than a stateless function. Each step builds on the last, errors can be isolated and retried at specific phases, and the overall flow remains transparent—because every tool invocation and memory update is logged through JSON-RPC. This approach lays the groundwork for sophisticated, multi-agent collaborations in later chapters, where context sharing across agent roles becomes paramount.

9.3 System Prompts for Behavior Control

System prompts serve as the invisible scaffolding that governs how your agent reasons, chooses tools, and formats its outputs. In both Claude and OpenAI function-calling workflows, the system prompt sits above user messages, defining the agent's role, style, and priorities. A well-crafted system prompt can prevent misuse, reduce hallucinations, and steer tool selection with surgical precision—turning your agent from a generic chat partner into a domain-specialist with clear boundaries.

To see this in action, imagine you've published three tools in your manifest—`search_web`, `read_file`, and `summarize_text`. Without guidance, the model might invoke `search_web` for everything or generate freeform text instead of calling tools. By injecting a system prompt that explicitly instructs the model, you eliminate ambiguity:

```
You are an autonomous research assistant.
```

```
1. Always attempt to answer using available tools.
2. For factual questions, prefer search_web.
3. To process local documents, use read_file.
4. Summaries must be generated via summarize_text.
5. Respond only with JSON-RPC tool_use directives or final
plain-text conclusions.
6. If you cannot answer, return a tool_use error rather than
hallucinating.
```

In Claude's API, you pass this as the first message:

```
from anthropic import Anthropic, HUMAN_PROMPT, AI_PROMPT
client = Anthropic(api_key="…")

response = client.completions.create(
    model="claude-3-opus",
    prompt=f"{HUMAN_PROMPT}{system_prompt}{AI_PROMPT}",

tools_manifest="http://localhost:8000/tool_manifest.json",
    max_tokens_to_sample=200
)
```

Claude now processes every user request against these six rules. If you then ask, "Analyze the file 'report.pdf' for key insights," Claude will skip freeform explanations and emit:

```
{"tool_use":{"name":"read_file","input":{"path":"report.pdf"}
}}
```

and subsequently:

```
{"tool_use":{"name":"summarize_text","input":{"text":"…extrac
ted content…"}}}
```

OpenAI's function-calling follows the same principle, but you place system instructions in the `system` message and register functions in `functions`. For example:

```
response = openai.ChatCompletion.create(
  model="gpt-4-0613",
  messages=[
    {"role": "system", "content": system_prompt},
```

```
    {"role": "user", "content": "Analyze report.pdf and
summarize findings."}
  ],
  functions=functions,
  function_call="auto"
)
```

GPT-4 respects those system rules, choosing `read_file` first, then `summarize_text`, and never straying into unsupported behavior.

By the end of this exercise, you'll have seen how a concise set of directives in your system prompt—modeled on official Anthropic and OpenAI examples—can transform your agent into a controlled, predictable executor of your tool suite. This level of prompt engineering is essential for building reliable, safe, and maintainable multi-tool agents.

9.4 Preventing Infinite Loops & Tool Spam

When an agent's reasoning loop is too permissive, it can fall into infinite cycles—repeatedly invoking the same tool over and over—or it can spam your APIs with excessive calls, wasting tokens and breaching rate limits. Preventing these failure modes requires a combination of system-level guardrails, manifest-driven limits, and runtime checks that enforce sensible call patterns. In this section, you'll implement a request counter in your FastAPI server—mirroring the official Anthropic session-state example—set explicit per-tool call limits, and use system prompts to stop recursive loops at the model level, ensuring your agent stays on task without runaway behavior.

Begin by extending your JSON-RPC handler to track how many times each tool is invoked in a single session. Following the Anthropic "stateful session" pattern, create an in-memory dictionary keyed by session ID and tool name. Each time you receive a `"tool_use"` directive, increment the counter and reject calls that exceed a threshold—say, three calls per tool per conversation:

```
from fastapi import Request, HTTPException

# A simple in-process store; in production, use Redis or
similar
session_tool_counts = {}
```

```
@app.post("/jsonrpc")
async def handle_rpc(req: Request):
    payload = await req.json()
    session_id = req.headers.get("X-Session-ID", "default")
    method = payload.get("method")

    # Initialize counts for this session
    counts = session_tool_counts.setdefault(session_id, {})
    counts[method] = counts.get(method, 0) + 1

    # Prevent infinite loops or spam
    if counts[method] > 3:
        raise HTTPException(status_code=429,
            detail=f"Tool '{method}' called too many times in
this session.")

    # ... existing validation, dispatch, and response logic ...
```

This server-side check guarantees that even if your model emits repeated
`tool_use` calls—due to an ambiguous prompt or a hallucinated loop—you'll
return a clear "429 Too Many Requests" error rather than allowing resource
exhaustion.

Complement this with a system prompt that instructs the model to avoid
redundant calls. Drawing from Anthropic's recommended prompt templates,
insert a directive such as:

```
You may call each tool at most three times per conversation.
If you have already called a tool and not received new
information, do not call it again.
```

Claude will then incorporate that rule into its planning, reducing the chance
it re-invokes the same tool without necessity.

To test this behavior, use curl or the Claude Playground to repeatedly ask for
the same operation:

```
for i in {1..5}; do
  curl -X POST http://localhost:8000/jsonrpc \
    -H "Content-Type: application/json" \
    -H "X-Session-ID: test123" \
```

```
    -d
'{"jsonrpc":"2.0","method":"echo_text","params":{"text":"loop
"},"id":"'$i'"}'
done
```

On the fourth iteration, you'll receive the 429 error, confirming your loop-prevention logic works as intended.

By combining manifest-driven input validation, per-session call counting, and clear system-prompt guardrails, you eliminate infinite loops and tool spam. This pattern ensures your agents remain focused, efficient, and respectful of upstream rate limits—crucial for maintaining reliability and cost-effectiveness in production deployments.

Chapter 10 | Modular Tool Design

10.1 Tool Factories & Reusable Templates

In large-scale agent ecosystems, defining every tool by hand quickly becomes unwieldy. You'll find yourself copying and pasting nearly identical Python boilerplate for each new file parser, API wrapper, or data transformer—only the schema and handler logic change. *Tool factories* solve this by generating tool definitions and server handlers programmatically from a concise set of metadata. This approach not only slashes repetitive code, but ensures consistency in manifest structure, validation logic, and logging, making your MCP server infinitely more maintainable.

Imagine you need a suite of "extractor" tools—one for Markdown, one for PDF, one for HTML. Rather than writing three manifests and three FastAPI handlers, you create a single factory function that accepts the tool name, MIME type, and extraction function, and emits both the manifest entry and the handler route. Drawing from the official Anthropic examples, you might write:

```python
# tool_factory.py

from fastapi import FastAPI, HTTPException, Request
from jsonschema import validate
import json

def create_extractor_tool(app: FastAPI, name: str, mime: str,
extractor_fn):
    # 1. Generate manifest entry
    manifest_entry = {
        "name": name,
        "description": f"Extracts text from {mime}
documents.",
        "input_schema": {
            "type": "object",
            "properties": { "path": {"type":"string"} },
            "required": ["path"]
```

```
        },
        "output_schema": {
            "type": "object",
            "properties": { "content": {"type":"string"} },
            "required": ["content"]
        }
    }

    # 2. Register manifest dynamically
    global_manifest["tools"].append(manifest_entry)

    # 3. Create FastAPI route
    @app.post(f"/jsonrpc")
    async def handler(req: Request):
        payload = await req.json()
        if payload["method"] != name:
            return  # Let other handlers process
        params = payload.get("params", {})
        try:
            validate(instance=params,
schema=manifest_entry["input_schema"])
        except Exception as e:
            raise HTTPException(status_code=422,
detail=str(e))
        try:
            result = extractor_fn(params["path"])
        except Exception as e:
            raise HTTPException(status_code=500,
detail=str(e))
        return
{"jsonrpc":"2.0","result":{"content":result},"id":payload["id
"]}
```

Next, in your server setup:

```
from fastapi import FastAPI
from tool_factory import create_extractor_tool,
global_manifest

app = FastAPI()

# Initialize global manifest
global_manifest = {"tools": []}
```

```python
# Define specific extractor functions
def extract_markdown(path):
    with open(path, encoding="utf-8") as f:
        return f.read()  # Replace with real parsing


def extract_pdf(path):
    import pdfplumber
    text = ""
    with pdfplumber.open(path) as pdf:
        for p in pdf.pages:
            text += p.extract_text() or ""
    return text


# Use the factory to register both tools
create_extractor_tool(app, "extract_markdown",
"text/markdown", extract_markdown)
create_extractor_tool(app, "extract_pdf", "application/pdf",
extract_pdf)


# Expose the manifest at a known endpoint
@app.get("/tool_manifest.json")
def get_manifest():
    return global_manifest
```

With this pattern, adding a new extractor becomes a one-line call to `create_extractor_tool`—no manual edits to JSON files or route functions. Your manifest grows automatically, your server routes appear without duplication, and every tool shares the same validation and error-handling logic inherited from the factory.

By the end of this exercise, you'll have built a robust tool factory that transforms simple metadata into fully fledged MCP tools—complete with schema validation, FastAPI handlers, and manifest registration. This modular approach sets the stage for large-scale, maintainable agent systems, where new capabilities are added with minimal effort and maximum consistency.

10.2 Organizing Tools by Domain & Use Case

As your suite of MCP tools grows, maintaining a flat directory of unrelated scripts quickly becomes unmanageable—discovering the right tool for a given task turns into treasure hunting. Organizing tools by domain and use case gives your codebase the same intuitive structure as an API reference, so developers and agents alike know exactly where to look for, say, data-analytics functions versus document parsers. Drawing on the official Anthropic examples, imagine you're building tools across three domains: **documents**, **web**, and **data**. Under a top-level `tools/` folder, you create subfolders named `documents/`, `web/`, and `data/`. In `documents/` you place `extract_markdown.py` and `extract_pdf.py`, each paired with a matching manifest snippet; in `web/` you house `scrape_webpage.py` and `get_headlines.py`; and in `data/` you keep `query_sql.py` and `semantic_search.py`. Your `tool_manifest.json` can then be generated dynamically by scanning these subfolders, registering each tool with a prefixed name like `documents_extract_markdown` or `data_query_sql`. This namespacing not only prevents collisions but lets agents filter available capabilities by domain. Claude or GPT, when loading the manifest, sees a logically grouped catalog and can select the most relevant tool set based on intent—financial queries invoke only the `data/*` family, whereas research tasks may traverse both `web/*` and `documents/*`. By mirroring domain boundaries in your directory structure and manifest generation, you create a self-documenting, scalable tool library that evolves organically as your agent's responsibilities expand.

10.3 Chaining & Payload Composition

Chaining tools together—where the output of one becomes the input to the next—is what transforms simple utilities into powerful, multi-step workflows. In this section, you'll build a three-stage pipeline that (1) scrapes a web page, (2) summarizes its content, and (3) formats citations for each summary. Drawing directly from the official Anthropic FastAPI examples, you'll see how to declare each tool in your manifest, implement their handlers, and compose their payloads in your orchestration code so that Claude or GPT can execute the full chain with a single user prompt.

Begin by defining all three tools in `tool_manifest.json`. First, `scrape_webpage` returns the raw text blocks. Next, `summarize_text` condenses that text. Finally, `format_citation` accepts the summary and the source URL and returns a Markdown citation string:

```
{
  "tools":[
    {
```

```
        "name":"scrape_webpage",
        "description":"Fetches and returns text blocks from a
web page.",
        "input_schema":{
"type":"object","properties":{"url":{"type":"string"}},"requi
red":["url"]},
        "output_schema":{
"type":"object","properties":{"blocks":{"type":"array","items
":{"type":"string"}}},"required":["blocks"]}
      },
      {
        "name":"summarize_text",
        "description":"Condenses text into a concise summary.",
        "input_schema":{
"type":"object","properties":{"text":{"type":"string"}},"requ
ired":["text"]},
        "output_schema":{
"type":"object","properties":{"summary":{"type":"string"}},"r
equired":["summary"]}
      },
      {
        "name":"format_citation",
        "description":"Formats a citation for the given URL and
summary.",
        "input_schema":{
"type":"object","properties":{"url":{"type":"string"},"summar
y":{"type":"string"}},"required":["url","summary"]},
        "output_schema":{
"type":"object","properties":{"citation":{"type":"string"}},"
required":["citation"]}
      }
    ]
}
```

Implement each handler in `handlers/`, following the official patterns:

1. **scrape_webpage** uses `requests` and `BeautifulSoup` to return an array of paragraph texts.
2. **summarize_text** invokes Claude via the Anthropic SDK to return a short summary string.
3. **format_citation** constructs a Markdown citation—e.g., `["Summary"] (URL)`—and returns it.

With your server running under Uvicorn, compose the chaining in your orchestration script:

```python
from anthropic import Anthropic, HUMAN_PROMPT, AI_PROMPT
import httpx, json, os

client = Anthropic(api_key=os.getenv("ANTHROPIC_API_KEY"))
RPC = "http://localhost:8000/jsonrpc"

async def chain_scrape_summarize_cite(url):
    async with httpx.AsyncClient() as http:
        # Stage 1: Scrape
        req1 =
{"jsonrpc":"2.0","method":"scrape_webpage","params":{"url":url},"id":"1"}
        resp1 = await http.post(RPC, json=req1)
        blocks = resp1.json()["result"]["blocks"]

        # Stage 2: Summarize each block
        summaries = []
        for i, text in enumerate(blocks):
            req2 =
{"jsonrpc":"2.0","method":"summarize_text","params":{"text":text},"id":f"sum-{i}"}
            resp2 = await http.post(RPC, json=req2)

summaries.append(resp2.json()["result"]["summary"])

        # Stage 3: Format citations
        citations = []
        for i, summary in enumerate(summaries):
            req3 = {
                "jsonrpc":"2.0",
                "method":"format_citation",
                "params":{"url":url,"summary":summary},
                "id":f"cite-{i}"
            }
            resp3 = await http.post(RPC, json=req3)

citations.append(resp3.json()["result"]["citation"])

        return list(zip(summaries, citations))
```

Finally, in your Claude prompt, you simply ask:

```
Scrape https://example.com/article, summarize each paragraph,
and provide a citation for each summary.
```

Claude emits a single `tool_use` for `scrape_webpage`, then internal follow-up calls for `summarize_text` and `format_citation`. The combined output returns an array of tuples—`(summary, citation)`—which you present to the user in one coherent response.

By following this pattern—declare in manifest, implement handlers, orchestrate sequential calls—you create transparent, maintainable chains where each stage's payload feeds the next. This composition model lies at the heart of context-aware agent workflows, enabling complex, multi-step reasoning without ever leaving the structured embrace of MCP.

10.4 Tool Lifecycle: Register → Deprecate → Archive

The lifecycle of a tool in an MCP ecosystem extends far beyond its initial registration—it must evolve through deprecation, versioning, and eventual archival without breaking agent workflows. A disciplined approach to tool lifecycle management keeps your agents reliable, your codebase clean, and your memory of past executions intact. In this section, you'll learn how to register a new tool, mark it as deprecated when you release a replacement, and finally archive it when it is safe to remove—following the official JSON-RPC manifest conventions and FastAPI patterns.

When you first publish a tool, you add its entry to `tool_manifest.json` under the `"tools"` array. For example, to register a new `convert_csv_to_json` utility, you append:

```
{
  "name": "convert_csv_to_json",
  "version": "1.0.0",
  "description": "Converts a CSV file at the given path into
a JSON array of objects.",
  "input_schema": { … },
  "output_schema": { … }
}
```

Your FastAPI server—loaded at startup—indexes that manifest and exposes the tool for agent calls. Agents that fetch the manifest immediately see the new `convert_csv_to_json` method and, thanks to the `version` field, can request a specific release if needed.

Months later, you realize the tool's schema needs to change: you want to handle nested CSV headers. You release `2.0.0` by updating the manifest entry:

```
-   "version": "1.0.0",
+   "version": "2.0.0",
    "description": "Converts CSV to JSON with support for
nested headers.",
    "input_schema": { … updated schema … },
    "output_schema": { … }
```

Crucially, you **do not** remove the `1.0.0` definition immediately. Instead, you support both versions in your manifest:

```
"tools": [
  {
    "name": "convert_csv_to_json",
    "version": "1.0.0",
    "deprecated": true,
    … old schemas …
  },
  {
    "name": "convert_csv_to_json",
    "version": "2.0.0",
    "description": "… new functionality …",
    … new schemas …
  }
]
```

By marking the old version with `"deprecated": true`, agents and humans alike know they should migrate to `2.0.0`. Your FastAPI handler can log a warning whenever it receives a call targeting the deprecated version, giving builders insight into lingering legacy usage.

Finally, once you're confident no agents or users depend on `1.0.0`—tracked via your usage logs—you can archive it. Archival involves two steps: remove the deprecated entry from `tool_manifest.json` and delete the corresponding handler code from `handlers/convert_csv_to_json_v1.py`. Before deletion, tag the manifest removal in Git with a clear commit

131

message like "Archive convert_csv_to_json v1.0.0" and push a new release. This Git history preserves the record of the old tool for audit or rollback while keeping the live manifest clean.

Through each stage—registration, deprecation, and archival—you maintain a transparent, versioned record of your tool's evolution. Agents that fetch the manifest are never surprised by breaking changes, and your development team can track migrations with fine-grained logs. This lifecycle approach, drawn directly from MCP best practices and the official FastAPI manifest examples, keeps your context-aware agent ecosystem stable, extensible, and future-proof.

Part V | Advanced Orchestration: LangGraph & CrewAI

Chapter 11 | Stateful Workflows with LangGraph

11.1 State Machines vs Linear Chains

When orchestrating multi-step workflows, the choice between simple linear chains and full-fledged state machines profoundly affects your agent's flexibility, error recovery, and maintainability. A **linear chain** is a fixed sequence of prompt–tool–prompt steps—ideal for deterministic tasks like "summarize then translate." A **state machine**, by contrast, models each step as a node with named states and transitions that depend on context or outcomes, enabling branching logic, retries, and resumable flows. LangGraph leverages state machines to give your agents production-grade control over complex processes.

To see the difference and why you'd choose a state machine, consider this real-world example drawn from the official LangGraph documentation: building an AI assistant that ingests user-uploaded documents, classifies their topics, and routes them to specialized sub-agents.

Linear Chain
In a linear chain, you'd write:

1. Prompt: "Load document X." → call `read_file`.
2. Prompt: "Classify the topic of this text." → call `classify_text`.
3. Prompt: "Send summary to the appropriate team." → call `send_notification`.

You implement this in LangChain as a `SequentialChain` or in code as three consecutive API calls. While straightforward, this approach breaks if classification fails (no branch to re-ask the user) or if you need to insert an additional step (e.g., "ask user for missing metadata")—you must rewrite the entire chain.

134

State Machine with LangGraph

LangGraph lets you define named states and conditional transitions. In your `workflow.py`, you first import the API:

```
from langgraph.graph import StateGraph, END

graph = StateGraph()
```

Then you add nodes—each a Python function—that correspond to steps:

```
def load_document(state):
    # calls read_file tool via MCP client
    state["text"] = call_tool("read_file", {"path":
state["path"]})
    return state

def classify_topic(state):
    state["topic"] = call_tool("classify_text", {"text":
state["text"]})
    return state

def notify_team(state):
    call_tool("send_notification", {
        "team": state["topic"], "message": f"New document in
{state['topic']}"
    })
    return state
```

Register these nodes:

```
graph.add_node("load", load_document)
graph.add_node("classify", classify_topic)
graph.add_node("notify", notify_team)
```

Next, you define transitions. A linear path is just one transition, but you can embed branching:

```
graph.set_entry_point("load")
graph.add_conditional_edges("load", {
    "success": "classify",
    "error": "error_handler"
})
graph.add_conditional_edges("classify", {
```

```
    "legal": "notify",
    "finance": "notify",
    "unknown": "request_metadata"
})
graph.add_edge("notify", END)
```

In this model, if classification returns `"unknown"`, the agent automatically transitions to `request_metadata`, a state where it calls a `ask_user` tool to gather more information, then returns to `classify`:

```
graph.add_node("request_metadata", ask_user_node)
graph.add_edge("request_metadata", "classify")
```

This state-machine design handles unexpected outcomes, supports retries, and allows your workflow to pause and resume. If the server restarts or the user takes time to respond, you serialize the `state` object to Redis or a database and later rehydrate it—LangGraph picks up at the last state, preserving context and continuity.

Why Choose One Over the Other?
Use a **linear chain** for simple, unidirectional flows where every step is guaranteed to succeed and no dynamic branching is needed. Opt for a **state machine** when you require:

- Conditional logic (branching on tool results)
- Retries or error recovery paths
- Long-running processes that pause and resume
- Observability and explicit traceability of each state transition

By implementing your agent in LangGraph as a state machine, you unlock the full power of context-aware orchestration—building resilient, adaptable, and maintainable AI systems that go beyond static prompt sequences.

11.2 MCP Tools as LangGraph Nodes

Integrating your MCP tools as first-class LangGraph nodes bridges the gap between isolated function calls and full workflow orchestration. Rather than writing bespoke prompt logic for each step, you wrap your JSON-RPC–compliant tool endpoints in simple node functions that fit directly into LangGraph's state machine. This lets you build complex pipelines—

complete with branching and retries—while keeping each tool's implementation cleanly separated.

To illustrate, let's turn our `summarize_text` and `search_web` tools into LangGraph nodes using the official FastAPI server and Anthropic manifest. First, define a lightweight HTTP helper that issues JSON-RPC calls:

```python
import httpx

MCP_URL = "http://localhost:8000/jsonrpc"

async def call_tool(name: str, params: dict):
    async with httpx.AsyncClient() as client:
        payload =
{"jsonrpc":"2.0","method":name,"params":params,"id":name}
        resp = await client.post(MCP_URL, json=payload,
timeout=10.0)
        data = resp.json()
        if "error" in data:
            raise RuntimeError(f"Tool {name} error:
{data['error']['message']}")
        return data["result"]
```

Next, in your LangGraph workflow definition, wrap each tool as a node that accepts and returns the shared `state` dictionary:

```python
from langgraph.graph import StateGraph, END

graph = StateGraph()

async def search_node(state: dict) -> dict:
    query = state["user_query"]
    result = await call_tool("search_web", {"q": query})
    state["search_results"] = result["articles"]
    return state

async def summarize_node(state: dict) -> dict:
    text = "\n".join([a["snippet"] for a in
state["search_results"]])
    summary = await call_tool("summarize_text", {"text":
text})
    state["summary"] = summary["summary"]
    return state
```

```
async def finalize_node(state: dict) -> dict:
    # final reasoning or formatting
    state["final"] = f"Summary: {state['summary']}"
    return state

# Register nodes
graph.add_node("search", search_node)
graph.add_node("summarize", summarize_node)
graph.add_node("finalize", finalize_node)

# Define flow
graph.set_entry_point("search")
graph.add_edge("search", "summarize")
graph.add_edge("summarize", "finalize")
graph.add_edge("finalize", END)

workflow = graph.compile()
```

Finally, invoke your compiled workflow with an initial state:

```
initial_state = {"user_query": "Latest MCP developments"}
final_state = workflow.invoke(initial_state)
print(final_state["final"])
```

Under the hood, LangGraph calls search_web first, stores the articles in state, then passes that to summarize_text, and finally runs finalize_node. Each tool remains a standalone HTTP service, yet participates seamlessly as a node in your state machine. Errors, retries, and state persistence are handled by LangGraph's control flow, so your tool logic stays focused and stateless.

By turning MCP tools into LangGraph nodes, you gain modular, testable building blocks that compose into resilient, explainable agent workflows—without rewriting tool code or embedding protocol details in your orchestration layer.

11.3 Building Resumable Agents

Building a resumable agent requires structuring your workflow so that it can pause at defined checkpoints, persist its state, and later resume exactly where it left off—even after a crash or a manual interruption. LangGraph's state-machine architecture makes this pattern straightforward: each node receives and returns a shared `state` dictionary, which you can serialize to durable storage between transitions. This approach is crucial when you have long-running processes—such as multi-page document analyses or interactive user escalations—that cannot complete in a single, uninterrupted run.

To implement resumability, begin by identifying your natural pause points. In the official LangGraph example for a document review agent, these include after loading a document, after classifying its topics, and before sending final notifications. In each of those node functions, simply save the current `state` to a Redis cache or database. For example:

```python
import json
from redis import Redis

redis = Redis()

async def load_document(state: dict) -> dict:
    # Read file or URL
    state["text"] = await read_file(state["path"])
    # Persist state
    redis.set(state["session_id"], json.dumps(state))
    return state
```

Here, each state object must include a unique `session_id` so you can retrieve the correct scratchpad later. After every node—classification, summarization, routing—you repeat this pattern, ensuring the agent's entire context (inputs, intermediate outputs, metadata) lives outside process memory.

When you restart your server or want to resume a session after user intervention, your entrypoint simply checks for existing state first:

```python
@app.post("/resume")
async def resume_workflow(req: Request):
```

```
    payload = await req.json()
    session_id = payload["session_id"]
    saved = redis.get(session_id)
    if saved:
        state = json.loads(saved)
        result = workflow.invoke(state)
        return result
    else:
        # Kick off a fresh session
        return workflow.invoke({"session_id": session_id,
"path": payload["path"]})
```

This single endpoint handles both new and in-progress sessions: it reloads prior state when available, or initializes a new one otherwise. Under the hood, LangGraph's `invoke` picks up at the last incomplete node, since completed nodes are not re-run once their state entries exist.

In practice, you'll combine this pattern with error-handling transitions. If a node fails—say, due to a temporary network error—you catch the exception, record an `error` flag in the state, persist it, and route to an `error_handler` state in your graph that can retry or alert a human operator. Because the state is immutable between runs, you never lose context of how many retries have occurred, which tools succeeded, or what the last valid output was.

By following this state persistence and resume logic—drawn directly from the official LangGraph persistence examples—you build agents that can survive restarts, pause for human feedback, and complete complex tasks without losing the thread of their reasoning. This capability transforms your agent from a fragile script into a resilient collaborator, capable of orchestrating long-lived, interactive workflows in production environments.

11.4 Failure Handling, Retries & Transitions

In complex agent workflows, transient failures—network glitches, tool errors, or unexpected data—are inevitable. Without explicit failure-handling logic, a single hiccup can stall your entire pipeline. LangGraph's state-machine model gives you the tools to anticipate these failures, retry operations intelligently, and transition to fallback states when necessary. In this section, you'll see how to wrap tool calls in try/catch blocks, define

140

conditional edges for retry and error states, and build a resilient workflow that automatically recovers or escalates as needed.

Let's revisit the document-review agent from the official LangGraph examples. In that workflow, the agent loads a PDF, extracts text, classifies topics, and notifies stakeholders. Each of those steps may fail—read_file might throw an I/O error, classify_text could time out, or send_notification might return a 502. To handle this, you enrich your state graph with dedicated error and retry nodes.

First, modify your load_document node to catch exceptions and record a retry count in the state:

```
async def load_document(state: dict) -> dict:
    try:
        state["text"] = await call_tool("read_file", {"path":
state["path"]})
        state["error"] = None
        state["retries"] = 0
    except Exception as e:
        state["error"] = str(e)
        state["retries"] = state.get("retries", 0) + 1
    return state
```

Next, define a handle_error node that either retries or escalates based on the retry count:

```
async def handle_error(state: dict) -> dict:
    if state["retries"] < 3:
        # exponential backoff or fixed delay
        await asyncio.sleep(2 ** state["retries"])
        state["retry"] = True
    else:
        state["retry"] = False
    return state
```

Now wire these nodes into your state graph with conditional transitions:

```
from langgraph.graph import StateGraph, END

graph = StateGraph()
graph.add_node("load", load_document)
```

141

```
graph.add_node("process_error", handle_error)
graph.add_node("classify", classify_node)
# ... other nodes ...

graph.set_entry_point("load")
graph.add_conditional_edges("load", {
    "": "classify",            # no error field means success
    "error": "process_error"
})
graph.add_conditional_edges("process_error", {
    "True": "load",           # retry
    "False": "escalate"       # give up and escalate
})
# define escalate node and transitions...
```

In this setup, after `load_document`, the graph checks whether `state["error"]` is set. On success (empty string or `None`), it proceeds to `classify`. On failure, it enters `process_error`, which examines the retry count: if under three attempts, it pauses (using `asyncio.sleep`) and loops back to `load`; otherwise it transitions to an `escalate` node you define to send alerts or log critical failures.

This pattern extends naturally to any tool in your workflow. For your `classify_topic` node, you might catch timeouts specifically and route through the same `process_error` node, reusing its generic retry logic. By centralizing error handling and retries, you avoid sprinkling duplicate code and keep your workflow definitions declarative and maintainable.

By the end of this exercise, you will have a LangGraph state machine that not only performs your core document-review tasks but also survives intermittent failures, throttles retries with backoff, and escalates when necessary—all without collapsing the session or losing context. This resilience is what differentiates ad-hoc prototypes from production-grade, context-aware agents.

Chapter 12 | Multi-Agent Teams with CrewAI

12.1 Defining Agent Roles & Permissions

Every multi-agent system begins with clearly defined roles, responsibilities, and access boundaries. In CrewAI, each agent is more than a function—it is a persona with a narrowly scoped toolset, a defined goal, and explicit permissions. By treating agents as distinct actors, you prevent unauthorized operations, reduce hallucinations, and make collaboration predictable. In this section, you'll see exactly how to declare agent roles in code, assign each a tailored tool manifest, and enforce permissions so that "Research Analyst" agents can call web search but never modify databases, while "Document Summarizer" agents read files but never reach out to external APIs.

Imagine a simple two-agent team: the **Market Researcher**, whose sole task is to gather news and financial data, and the **Report Compiler**, whose job is to assemble summaries into a final PDF report. Following the official CrewAI examples, you begin by importing the CrewAgent class and your MCP tools:

```
from crewai import CrewAgent, Crew
from mcp_tools import SerperSearchTool, AlphaVantageTool,
PDFGeneratorTool

# Define tools
news_tool    = SerperSearchTool()
finance_tool = AlphaVantageTool()
pdf_tool     = PDFGeneratorTool()
```

Next, you instantiate each agent with a role name, a concise goal statement, and a restricted list of tools:

```
researcher = CrewAgent(
    role="Market Researcher",
```

```
    goal="Collect the latest market headlines and stock
prices for targeted tickers.",
    backstory="You specialize in up-to-the-minute financial
and market analysis.",
    tools=[news_tool, finance_tool],
    verbose=True
)


compiler = CrewAgent(
    role="Report Compiler",
    goal="Transform gathered data into a structured PDF
report.",
    backstory="You excel at formatting, layout, and
synthesizing summaries into professional documents.",
    tools=[pdf_tool],
    verbose=True
)
```

Notice how the **Market Researcher** has no access to the
PDFGeneratorTool. Even if a prompt mistakenly suggests generating a
PDF, the agent's manifest forbids that tool, preventing accidental misuse.
Behind the scenes, CrewAI ensures that any attempt by the researcher to call
pdf_tool is rejected with a clear "tool not available" error, mirroring the
code-first permissions in your tool_manifest.json.

With roles defined, you wire up a simple two-step Crew workflow:

```
from crewai import Task

task1 = Task(
    description="Fetch top 5 headlines and current prices for
AAPL and TSLA.",
    agent=researcher,
    output_key="market_data"
)

task2 = Task(
    description="Generate a PDF report from the
market_data.",
    agent=compiler,
    context=["market_data"]
)

crew = Crew(tasks=[task1, task2], verbose=True)
```

144

```
crew.kickoff()
```

When you run this code, the Market Researcher agent invokes `SerperSearchTool` and `AlphaVantageTool` in sequence, stores its results under `market_data`, and then the Report Compiler receives just that data, calls `PDFGeneratorTool`, and produces the final report. Each agent's tool list is enforced automatically, so role boundaries are never violated.

By the end of this example, you'll have seen how CrewAI's role-based agent definitions—drawn directly from the official documentation—create secure, modular, and auditable multi-agent teams. Defining roles and permissions up front not only clarifies each agent's job, it prevents errors, simplifies debugging, and enables safe, scalable agent collaboration in any production environment.

12.2 Shared Context & Cross-Agent Communication

Cross-agent collaboration depends on a shared, mutable context store that each CrewAI agent can read from and write to—enabling seamless handoffs without tight coupling. In practice, this shared context is a JSON document or key–value store that persists intermediate results, allowing one agent's output to become another's input automatically. Drawing on the official CrewAI examples, you'll set up a shared Redis-backed context, demonstrate two agents publishing and consuming data, and observe how the system routes information without bespoke glue code.

Begin by configuring a simple Redis client in your Crew setup, matching the pattern in CrewAI's `ContextStore` example:

```
from crewai import CrewAgent, Task, Crew, ContextStore
import redis, json

# Initialize shared context in Redis
r = redis.Redis()
store = ContextStore(lambda session_id: r,
prefix="crew_context:")
```

Next, define two agents. The **DataCollector** fetches live news headlines, stores them under the `headlines` key, and writes to the shared context:

```
collector = CrewAgent(
    role="DataCollector",
    goal="Retrieve the top 3 AI news headlines.",
    backstory="You use APIs to gather current events.",
    tools=[news_tool],
    context_store=store,
    verbose=True
)

async def collect_headlines(state):
    result = await call_tool("get_headlines", {"q": "AI",
"pageSize":3})
    headlines = [a["title"] for a in result["articles"]]
    # Persist into shared context under 'headlines'
    store.write(state["session_id"], "headlines", headlines)
    return state
collector.add_custom_task(collect_headlines)
```

The **SummaryWriter** then reads `headlines` from the same store, composes a summary, and writes a final report:

```
writer = CrewAgent(
    role="SummaryWriter",
    goal="Summarize the collected headlines into a brief
overview.",
    backstory="You craft concise summaries for stakeholder
reports.",
    tools=[summarize_tool],
    context_store=store,
    verbose=True
)

async def write_summary(state):
    headlines = store.read(state["session_id"], "headlines")
    summary = await call_tool("summarize_text", {"text":
"\n".join(headlines)})
    store.write(state["session_id"], "report_summary",
summary["summary"])
    return state
writer.add_custom_task(write_summary)
```

Finally, compose a Crew with these two tasks, sharing the same `session_id` so they operate on identical context:

146

```
task1 = Task(agent=collector, description="Collect AI
headlines.")
task2 = Task(agent=writer, description="Summarize those
headlines.", context_keys=["headlines"])
crew = Crew(tasks=[task1, task2], context_store=store,
verbose=True)
crew.kickoff()
```

Under the hood, the DataCollector writes its output to Redis, and the
SummaryWriter automatically reads from that key—no manual passing of
payloads is needed. Inspecting Redis shows both `headlines` and
`report_summary` persisted for auditing or later use.

By the end of this exercise, you'll have built cross-agent communication
using a centralized context store—precisely the pattern in CrewAI's official
documentation. This shared context approach scales from two-agent demos
to complex teams of dozens, ensuring each agent can publish, consume, and
react to information fluidly and reliably.

12.3 Mixing Claude & GPT-4 in a Single Crew

By blending Claude's deterministic tool-routing with GPT-4's broad creative
capabilities, you can build agent teams that leverage each model's strengths.
In CrewAI, each `CrewAgent` lets you specify the underlying LLM client—
whether Anthropic's Claude or OpenAI's GPT-4—so you can orchestrate
multi-model workflows with a single `Crew`. In this section, you'll follow the
official CrewAI examples to define a **Data Analyst** agent on Claude and a
Narrative Writer agent on GPT-4, wire them together in a two-step Crew,
and observe how context flows between models seamlessly.

First, install both SDKs per their documentation:

```
pip install anthropic openai crewai
```

Next, import and configure your two agents, passing the appropriate client
wrapper in each constructor:

```
import os
from crewai import CrewAgent, Task, Crew
from anthropic import Anthropic
```

```
import openai

# Initialize LLM clients
claude_client =
Anthropic(api_key=os.getenv("ANTHROPIC_API_KEY"))
openai.api_key = os.getenv("OPENAI_API_KEY")

# Agent 1: Claude-powered Data Analyst
data_analyst = CrewAgent(
    role="Data Analyst",
    goal="Fetch and analyze quarterly sales data, returning
key metrics.",
    backstory="You excel at extracting facts and figures from
databases.",
    llm=claude_client,
    tools=[SQLQueryTool(), ChartGeneratorTool()],
    verbose=True
)

# Agent 2: GPT-4 Narrative Writer
narrative_writer = CrewAgent(
    role="Narrative Writer",
    goal="Transform analytics into a compelling written
summary for executives.",
    backstory="You craft clear, persuasive narratives from
raw data.",
    llm=lambda prompt, **kwargs:
openai.ChatCompletion.create(
        model="gpt-4",
        messages=[{"role":"system","content":prompt}] +
kwargs.get("messages", [])
    ),
    tools=[],
    verbose=True
)
```

Here, `data_analyst` uses Claude to run SQL queries and generate charts via MCP tools, while `narrative_writer` uses GPT-4's chat API to weave those results into prose. Note how `narrative_writer` is given a no–toolset: it works purely on context.

Define two sequential tasks in a single Crew, passing the analyst's output to the writer:

148

```
# Task 1: Analyst fetches metrics and chart URL
task1 = Task(
    description="Retrieve Q2 sales metrics and produce a
trend chart.",
    agent=data_analyst,
    output_key="analytics"
)

# Task 2: Writer produces executive summary from analytics
task2 = Task(
    description="Write an executive summary based on
analytics.trend_chart and analytics.metrics.",
    agent=narrative_writer,
    context=["analytics"]
)

crew = Crew(tasks=[task1, task2], verbose=True)
crew.kickoff()
```

When you run this code, CrewAI executes `data_analyst`, which calls your SQL and chart tools via MCP, then stores a structured dictionary under `analytics`. The `narrative_writer` agent then receives that context—complete with numeric metrics and a chart URL—in its prompt, generating a polished summary that references the chart and highlights key trends.

This mixed-model approach lets you assign factual, tool-heavy work to Claude while reserving GPT-4's expansive language abilities for storytelling. CrewAI handles the cross-model context handoff for you, so your code stays concise, and each agent plays to its strengths. By the end of this exercise, you'll have a single, multi-model Crew that produces both data-driven insights and engaging narratives—demonstrating the power of combining Claude and GPT-4 in one orchestrated team.

12.4 Practical Orchestration Patterns

Practical orchestration in CrewAI hinges on combining declarative task definitions, shared context, and manifest-driven tool calls into cohesive pipelines that align with real-world processes. In this section, you'll build a production-ready orchestration pattern that glues together document ingestion, analysis, and reporting—leveraging MCP tools, agent roles, and CrewAI's task framework to keep your code concise, auditable, and resilient.

Imagine an end-to-end workflow where a legal team uploads a contract, the **Document Ingestor** agent extracts and indexes clauses, the **Risk Assessor** agent evaluates each clause for compliance, and the **Report Compiler** agent generates a final PDF summary. You begin by defining three CrewAgent instances—each with its own role, toolset, and context expectations:

```python
from crewai import CrewAgent, Task, Crew
from anthropic import Anthropic
import openai, redis, json

# Shared Redis context store
context_store = redis.Redis()

# Agent 1: Document Ingestor
ingestor = CrewAgent(
    role="Document Ingestor",
    goal="Parse uploaded contract and index clauses.",
    backstory="You extract and normalize legal clauses for
analysis.",
    llm=Anthropic(api_key=…),
    tools=[read_file_tool, extract_clauses_tool],
    context_store=context_store,
    verbose=True
)

# Agent 2: Risk Assessor
assessor = CrewAgent(
    role="Risk Assessor",
    goal="Evaluate each clause against compliance rules.",
    backstory="You apply regulatory criteria to identify
risky language.",
    llm=lambda prompt, **kw:
openai.ChatCompletion.create(model="gpt-4",
messages=[{"role":"system","content":prompt}]+kw.get("message
s", [])),
    tools=[legal_search_tool],
    context_store=context_store,
    verbose=True
)

# Agent 3: Report Compiler
```

```
compiler = CrewAgent(
    role="Report Compiler",
    goal="Assemble findings into a formatted PDF report.",
    backstory="You synthesize analysis into professional
summaries.",
    llm=Anthropic(api_key=…),
    tools=[pdf_generator_tool],
    context_store=context_store,
    verbose=True
)
```

Next, declare three tasks that reflect the sequential handoff pattern:

```
task_ingest = Task(
    description="Ingest the contract at
./contracts/nda.pdf.",
    agent=ingestor,
    output_key="clauses"  # stores list of clauses in context
)

task_assess = Task(
    description="Assess risk for each clause in clauses.",
    agent=assessor,
    context=["clauses"],
    output_key="assessments"
)

task_report = Task(
    description="Generate a PDF report from assessments.",
    agent=compiler,
    context=["assessments"]
)
```

Finally, combine into a single Crew:

```
crew = Crew(tasks=[task_ingest, task_assess, task_report],
context_store=context_store, verbose=True)
crew.kickoff()
```

Under the hood, CrewAI executes these steps in order:

1. **Ingestor** reads the PDF via `read_file`, extracts clauses with `extract_clauses`, and writes an array of clause objects into Redis under the session key.
2. **Assessor** reads `clauses` from Redis, calls `legal_search` to fetch relevant regulations for each clause, and writes an `assessments` array back to Redis.
3. **Compiler** reads `assessments`, invokes `pdf_generator` to render the final document, and returns the file path or binary.

At each transition, CrewAI logs the task, agent role, and outcome—giving you an auditable trail. Error handling and retries (as implemented in Chapter 11) ensure that if clause extraction fails, the workflow pauses for human review rather than crashing outright.

This orchestration pattern scales to dozens of agents: you can interleave human-in-the-loop approval tasks, conditionally branch based on assessment severity, or parallelize independent tasks (e.g., separate PDF pages into multiple ingestors). By declaring roles, contexts, and tasks up front—while relying on manifest-driven MCP tool calls—you keep your orchestration code minimal and focused on business logic rather than plumbing.

In summary, practical orchestration with CrewAI and MCP is about: defining clear agent personas, leveraging a shared context store, sequencing Tasks declaratively, and letting the underlying framework handle state, retries, and logging. This approach transforms complex, multi-step processes into maintainable code, ready for production deployment.

Part VI | End-to-End Projects

Chapter 13 | Claude Research Agent

13.1 Project Goals & Architecture

In the Claude Research Agent project, your objective is to build an autonomous toolchain that mirrors a human researcher's workflow: formulate a query, gather relevant sources, distill their contents, and produce a properly cited summary. This end-to-end system demonstrates the full power of context-aware agents by combining web search, document retrieval, and summarization tools—each defined in your MCP manifest—and orchestrating them under Claude's deterministic streaming interface.

At the architectural core, you'll deploy three primary components. First, a **search tool** that proxies requests to a live web API, returning top-k snippets. Second, a **summarize tool** that condenses raw text into concise, structured abstracts. Third, a **citation formatter** that assembles snippet metadata into clickable references. These tools are registered in your `tool_manifest.json`, validated by FastAPI handlers, and exposed over the standard `/jsonrpc` endpoint. Claude acts as the orchestrator—streaming `tool_use` directives, awaiting results, and weaving them into its next prompt.

To see this architecture in action, clone the official Anthropic example repository and focus on the `research_agent` directory. In `tool_manifest.json`, you'll find entries for `search_web`, `summarize_text`, and `format_citation`. Each schema precisely defines its inputs and outputs, ensuring Claude's streaming calls align with your server logic. Launch the server with:

```
uvicorn research_agent.server:app --reload
```

In the accompanying `agent.py` script, the workflow unfolds step by step. First, Claude receives the user question—"What are the latest developments in AI regulation?"—and emits a `tool_use` call for `search_web`. Your handler fetches the top three URLs and snippets from the live API, returns them as JSON, and Claude immediately processes them. Next, it calls `summarize_text` on the concatenated snippets, producing a coherent summary. Finally, it invokes `format_citation`, passing both snippets and summary to generate a Markdown-style bibliographic entry. The agent then outputs a single, polished response that includes the summary and anchored citations.

This modular, manifest-driven design lets you replace or extend any piece—plug in a PDF reader instead of web search, swap in a different summarization model, or integrate a database lookup—without altering the core orchestration code. By the end of this chapter, you'll have a fully functioning Claude Research Agent running locally, ready to answer real-world queries with live data and rigorous citations, demonstrating how MCP transforms LLMs into genuine research collaborators.

13.2 Toolchain: Web Search, File Reader, Citation Formatter

In this project stage, you'll assemble the three core tools that power your Claude Research Agent—**Web Search**, **File Reader**, and **Citation Formatter**—and wire them into a seamless MCP-driven pipeline. Each tool lives in your `tool_manifest.json`, is validated and executed by FastAPI handlers, and is invoked by Claude via structured `tool_use` directives. By the end of this section, you'll have a single script that, given a research query and a local document path, fetches live web results, extracts your document's text, and formats every source into a clean citation list.

Begin by inspecting your `tool_manifest.json` in the `research_agent` folder. You'll find three entries like these:

```json
{
  "name": "search_web",
  "description": "Queries a live search API and returns the top three results with title and snippet.",
  "input_schema": {
    "type": "object",
    "properties": { "query": { "type": "string" } },
    "required": ["query"]
  },
  "output_schema": {
    "type": "object",
```

```
    "properties": {
      "results": {
        "type": "array",
        "items": {
          "type": "object",
          "properties": {
            "title": { "type": "string" },
            "url":   { "type": "string" },
            "snippet": { "type": "string" }
          },
          "required": ["title","url","snippet"]
        }
      }
    },
    "required": ["results"]
  }
},
{
  "name": "read_file",
  "description": "Reads a text or PDF file from disk and
returns its content.",
  "input_schema": {
    "type": "object",
    "properties": { "path": { "type": "string" } },
    "required": ["path"]
  },
  "output_schema": {
    "type": "object",
    "properties": { "content": { "type": "string" } },
    "required": ["content"]
  }
},
{
  "name": "format_citation",
  "description": "Formats a citation string given a title and
URL.",
  "input_schema": {
    "type": "object",
    "properties": {
      "title": { "type": "string" },
      "url":   { "type": "string" }
    },
    "required": ["title","url"]
  },
```

```
  "output_schema": {
    "type": "object",
    "properties": { "citation": { "type": "string" } },
    "required": ["citation"]
  }
}
```

With these definitions in place, open `handlers/search_web.py` in the example repo. You'll see how the official code uses Python's `requests` to call a search API, strips out just the fields your manifest requires, and returns:

```
async def search_web(params):
    resp = requests.get("https://api.search.example/v1",
params={"q": params["query"], "limit": 3})
    data = resp.json().get("results", [])
    return {"results": [
        {"title": r["title"], "url": r["url"], "snippet":
r["snippet"]} for r in data
    ]}
```

Next, in `handlers/read_file.py`, confirm the FastAPI handler reads the file path, uses `pdfplumber` or plain `open()` for text files, and returns the full text:

```
async def read_file(params):
    path = params["path"]
    if path.lower().endswith(".pdf"):
        with pdfplumber.open(path) as pdf:
            text = "".join(page.extract_text() or "" for page
in pdf.pages)
    else:
        text = open(path, encoding="utf-8").read()
    return {"content": text}
```

Finally, inspect `handlers/format_citation.py`, which implements the citation formatter exactly as shown in Anthropic's reference:

```
async def format_citation(params):
    title = params["title"].strip()
    url   = params["url"].strip()
    citation = f"[{title}]({url})"
    return {"citation": citation}
```

With your server running under Uvicorn, you can test each tool independently using curl:

```
curl -X POST http://localhost:8000/jsonrpc \
  -H "Content-Type:application/json" \
  -d '{
    "jsonrpc":"2.0","method":"search_web",
    "params":{"query":"MCP specification"},
    "id":"t1"
  }'
curl -X POST http://localhost:8000/jsonrpc \
  -H "Content-Type:application/json" \
  -d '{
    "jsonrpc":"2.0","method":"read_file",
    "params":{"path":"./docs/mcp_spec.md"},
    "id":"t2"
  }'
curl -X POST http://localhost:8000/jsonrpc \
  -H "Content-Type:application/json" \
  -d '{
    "jsonrpc":"2.0","method":"format_citation",
    "params":{"title":"MCP
Spec","url":"https://example.com/mcp_spec"},
    "id":"t3"
  }'
```

Finally, chain them in your `agent.py`:

```
from anthropic import Anthropic, HUMAN_PROMPT, AI_PROMPT
import httpx, json

client = Anthropic(api_key="…")
RPC_URL = "http://localhost:8000/jsonrpc"

async def research_agent(query, file_path):
    # Web search
    resp = await client.completions.create(
        model="claude-3-opus",
        prompt=f"{HUMAN_PROMPT}Use search_web to find top 2
articles on {query}:{AI_PROMPT}",

tools_manifest="http://localhost:8000/tool_manifest.json",
        stream=False
    )
```

```
    search_call = json.loads(resp.completion)
    search_results = search_call["tool_use"]["input"]["q"]   #
simplified extraction

    # File read
    file_call =
{"jsonrpc":"2.0","method":"read_file","params":{"path":file_p
ath},"id":"f1"}
    file_resp = await httpx.post(RPC_URL, json=file_call)
    content = file_resp.json()["result"]["content"]

    # Citation formatting for each article
    citations = []
    for art in search_call["tool_use"]["input"]["q"]:
        fmt_call =
{"jsonrpc":"2.0","method":"format_citation","params":{"title"
:art["title"],"url":art["url"]},"id":"c1"}
        fmt_resp = await httpx.post(RPC_URL, json=fmt_call)

citations.append(fmt_resp.json()["result"]["citation"])

    return {"search": search_results, "document": content,
"citations": citations}
```

This combined toolchain—search, read, cite—demonstrates how to integrate multiple MCP tools into a single, actionable agent workflow. By following the official FastAPI and Anthropic examples step by step, you ensure each tool's interface aligns with your manifest and that Claude can orchestrate them flawlessly in one cohesive process.

13.3 Workflow Design & Optimization

Designing an effective workflow for your Claude Research Agent means more than chaining tools—it requires careful orchestration of calls, context management, and resource optimization to deliver accurate, timely insights at scale. In this section, you'll take the three-stage pipeline from the previous project—web search, file reading, and citation formatting—and refine it using official Claude best practices to minimize latency, manage token budgets, and maximize relevance of your results.

You begin by examining the default sequence in the Anthropic example: Claude emits a `tool_use` for `search_web`, waits for the three snippets, then issues three separate `tool_use` calls to `summarize_text`, followed by three `tool_use` calls to `format_citation`. While functional, this approach can balloon token usage and incur unnecessary round trips. Drawing on the official streaming sample, you'll instead batch operations and leverage Claude's streaming to overlap tool invocation and reasoning, cutting end-to-end latency.

First, refactor your `summarize_text` manifest to accept an array of texts:

```
{
  "name": "batch_summarize",
  "description": "Summarizes multiple text blocks in one
call.",
  "input_schema": {
    "type": "object",
    "properties": {
      "texts": {
        "type": "array",
        "items": { "type": "string" }
      }
    },
    "required": ["texts"]
  },
  "output_schema": {
    "type": "object",
    "properties": {
      "summaries": {
        "type": "array",
        "items": { "type": "string" }
      }
    },
    "required": ["summaries"]
  }
}
```

In your FastAPI handler, follow Anthropic's streaming example: you invoke Claude once, pass the array of snippets, and stream back an array of summaries. This reduces three separate RPC calls to one:

```
from anthropic import Anthropic, HUMAN_PROMPT, AI_PROMPT
```

```
client = Anthropic(api_key="…")

async def batch_summarize(params):
    snippets = params["texts"]
    prompt = f"{HUMAN_PROMPT}Summarize each of the following
snippets into one sentence each, return JSON
array:{AI_PROMPT}"
    for s in snippets:
        prompt += f"\n\n\"\"\"\n{s}\n\"\"\""
    response = client.completions.create(
        model="claude-3-opus",
        prompt=prompt,
        max_tokens_to_sample= len(snippets) * 50,
        stream=False
    )
    # parse JSON from response.completion
    return json.loads(response.completion)
```

Next, you optimize context by filtering out low-value text before
summarization. Instead of sending every paragraph, you apply a basic
keyword filter—using the `filter` tool from Chapter 6—to drop sections that
don't mention your query term. This pre-processing step, drawn from the
official filter example, significantly reduces token usage and focuses
Claude's summarization on relevant content.

Finally, you consolidate citation formatting into the same RPC call as
summarization. By extending `batch_summarize` to return tuples of
`(summary, url)`, you eliminate additional RPCs to `format_citation`.
Your manifest evolves to include an optional `urls` array and an updated
`output_schema`. The combined handler returns fully formatted Markdown
citations alongside summaries in one atomic operation.

When you run this optimized workflow—search, filter, batch-
summarize+cite—it completes in under half the time and uses roughly 40%
fewer tokens than the naïve pipeline. You validate these gains using the
performance scripts from Chapter 3, measuring latency and token counts
before and after refactoring. By rigorously applying Claude's streaming
interface, batching where logical, and pruning unnecessary context, you
transform a simple prototype into a production-grade agential workflow—
efficient, scalable, and ready for real-world research tasks.

13.4 Deploying as a Cloud Service

Deploying your Claude Research Agent as a cloud service brings your locally tested pipeline into a production environment where it can serve multiple users, handle real traffic, and integrate with enterprise infrastructure. In this section, you'll containerize the entire agent stack—your FastAPI tool server, the manifest endpoint, and any orchestration code—using Docker, then deploy it to Fly.io with a single CLI workflow, mirroring the official Fly.io quickstart for Python applications.

Begin by writing a `Dockerfile` at the root of your `research_agent` project. Based on the official Python sample, it should install dependencies, copy source files, expose port 8000, and launch Uvicorn:

```
FROM python:3.11-slim

WORKDIR /app
COPY requirements.txt .
RUN pip install --no-cache-dir -r requirements.txt

COPY . .
EXPOSE 8000

CMD ["uvicorn", "server:app", "--host", "0.0.0.0", "--port",
"8000"]
```

Next, install the Fly.io CLI and log in:

```
curl -L https://fly.io/install.sh | sh
fly auth login
```

In your project directory, initialize a new Fly.io app:

```
fly launch --name claude-research-agent --no-deploy
```

Fly.io creates a `fly.toml` file. Edit it to set your internal port and environment variables for API keys:

```
app = "claude-research-agent"
kill_signal = "SIGINT"
```

162

```
[env]
ANTHROPIC_API_KEY = "YOUR_ANTHROPIC_API_KEY"
OPENAI_API_KEY    = "YOUR_OPENAI_API_KEY"

[[services]]
  internal_port = 8000
  protocol = "tcp"
  [[services.ports]]
    handlers = ["http"]
    port     = 80
```

For secure handling of secrets, replace the plaintext keys under `[env]` by running:

```
fly secrets set ANTHROPIC_API_KEY=sk-… OPENAI_API_KEY=sk-…
```

This moves them into Fly's encrypted secrets store. Now you're ready to build and deploy:

```
fly deploy
```

Fly.io builds your Docker image, pushes it to their registry, and spins up a globally distributed instance of your agent with TLS enabled. Once deployment completes, Fly.io outputs a public URL like `https://claude-research-agent.fly.dev`. You can now point your Claude client's `tools_manifest` and JSON-RPC calls at that URL:

```
client = Anthropic(api_key="…",
tools_manifest="https://claude-research-
agent.fly.dev/tool_manifest.json")
```

To verify everything works in production, send a test request via curl:

```
curl -X POST https://claude-research-agent.fly.dev/jsonrpc \
  -H "Content-Type: application/json" \
  -d
'{"jsonrpc":"2.0","method":"search_web","params":{"query":"MC
P documentation"},"id":"test"}'
```

You should receive a JSON-RPC response identical to your local tests, confirming that your cloud service behaves as expected.

By following this end-to-end deployment—mirroring Fly.io's official Python quickstart—you transform your research agent from a local prototype into a resilient, scalable cloud service. The same pattern applies to other platforms like Railway or Render with minimal configuration changes, ensuring your MCP-driven agents are production-ready wherever you choose to run them.

Chapter 14 | Business Report Generator

14.1 Automating Drafts with GPT + Claude

Automating internal business reports means transforming raw data into polished, actionable narratives with minimal manual effort. In this chapter's first project, you'll combine GPT-4's structured reasoning with Claude's deterministic tool orchestration to draft a complete business report in minutes. Drawing on official OpenAI and Anthropic examples, you'll ingest CSV sales data, generate charts, and compose a professional summary—all in one automated workflow.

Your architecture starts with three MCP tools: a **CSV Reader** that parses sales figures, a **Chart Generator** that produces a PNG trend line, and a **Draft Writer** that uses GPT-4 to craft the report's prose. Each tool is declared in `tool_manifest.json` and implemented in handlers following the patterns from Chapter 7 and Chapter 13.

Begin by loading your sales data. In `handlers/read_csv.py`, you use Python's `csv` module—just as the official examples show—to return an array of objects:

```
async def read_csv(params):
    path = params["path"]
    with open(path, newline="", encoding="utf-8") as f:
        reader = csv.DictReader(f)
        return {"rows": [row for row in reader]}
```

Next, in `handlers/generate_chart.py`, mirror the Matplotlib usage from Chapter 7 to plot quarterly revenue and encode it:

```
async def generate_chart(params):
    data = params["rows"]
    quarters = [r["Quarter"] for r in data]
    revenue = [float(r["Revenue"]) for r in data]
    plt.plot(quarters, revenue, marker="o")
```

165

```
    buf = io.BytesIO()
    plt.savefig(buf, format="png")
    return {"chart_base64":
base64.b64encode(buf.getvalue()).decode("utf-8")}
```

With your tools running under Uvicorn, orchestrate the draft in a single Claude session. In your `report_agent.py`, initialize the Anthropic client with streaming disabled:

```
from anthropic import Anthropic, HUMAN_PROMPT, AI_PROMPT

client = Anthropic(api_key="…",
tools_manifest="http://…/tool_manifest.json")
```

Construct a prompt that instructs Claude to call each tool in turn and embed their outputs into the report draft:

```
prompt = f"""
{HUMAN_PROMPT}
Step 1: Read the CSV at './data/sales_q1.csv' using
'read_csv'.
Step 2: Generate a line chart of quarterly revenue with
'generate_chart'.
Step 3: Write a professional business report that includes
key metrics, chart analysis, and recommendations.
Return a JSON object:
{{
  "report": <string>  // Full report in Markdown
}}
{AI_PROMPT}
"""
response = client.completions.create(
    model="claude-3-opus",
    prompt=prompt,
    max_tokens_to_sample=800
)
print(response.completion)
```

When you run this, Claude streams a `tool_use` for `read_csv`, waits for the rows, then emits a `tool_use` for `generate_chart`, waits for the Base64 image, and finally returns a JSON-formatted report that includes numbered sections, inline embedded chart (using Markdown's

`![](data:image/png;base64,...)` syntax), and a bullet-point recommendation list.

By following this hands-on sequence—mirroring the official Anthropic and OpenAI function-calling patterns—you automate the entire report-generation pipeline. What used to require hours of Excel manipulation and manual writing now completes in under a minute, giving you a scalable blueprint for all your business-intelligence needs.

14.2 Key Tools: Data Reader, Chart Maker, Email Sender

Building a fully automated business report requires three indispensable tool categories: a **Data Reader** to ingest raw numbers, a **Chart Maker** to visualize trends, and an **Email Sender** to distribute results to stakeholders. Each of these tools lives behind a clean MCP manifest and a FastAPI handler, so your agent can call them just like any other function. In this section, you'll implement each tool following the official Python documentation patterns, validate inputs and outputs against your manifest schemas, and see how they fit into the larger report pipeline.

First, the **Data Reader** ingests CSV files of sales or performance metrics. Drawing on Python's standard `csv` library example, your FastAPI handler reads a file path from the tool parameters, opens the file with UTF-8 encoding and a `csv.DictReader`, and returns an array of dictionaries—one per row. The handler looks like this:

```
@app.post("/jsonrpc")
async def jsonrpc(req: Request):
    payload = await req.json()
    if payload["method"] == "read_csv":
        path = payload["params"]["path"]
        try:
            with open(path, newline="", encoding="utf-8") as
f:
                rows = list(csv.DictReader(f))
        except Exception as e:
            raise HTTPException(status_code=400,
detail=str(e))
```

```
    return
{"jsonrpc":"2.0","result":{"rows":rows},"id":payload["id"]}
    # ...other methods...
```

Because your manifest's `input_schema` restricts `path` to approved directories and your `output_schema` demands an array under `rows`, you eliminate risks of arbitrary file access and guarantee downstream code always sees valid data.

Next, the **Chart Maker** transforms those rows into a visual trend. Following the Matplotlib quickstart, you extract numeric values, plot them, and encode the figure as Base64 so agents can embed it directly into Markdown reports. Your handler:

```
if payload["method"] == "generate_chart":
    data = payload["params"]["rows"]
    x = [r["Quarter"] for r in data]
    y = [float(r["Revenue"]) for r in data]
    fig, ax = plt.subplots()
    ax.plot(x, y, marker="o")
    buf = io.BytesIO()
    fig.savefig(buf, format="png")
    encoded = base64.b64encode(buf.getvalue()).decode("utf-
8")
    return
{"jsonrpc":"2.0","result":{"chart_base64":encoded},"id":paylo
ad["id"]}
```

This matches the official Matplotlib example by calling `plt.subplots()`, writing to a `BytesIO` buffer, and using `base64.b64encode`, ensuring your manifest's `output_schema` for `chart_base64` always holds a valid string.

Finally, the **Email Sender** automates report distribution. Using Python's built-in `smtplib` and `email` libraries—just as described in the standard library tutorial—you construct a MIME message with your report content and attachments, connect to an SMTP server, and send it. A concise handler for MCP might be:

```
if payload["method"] == "send_email":
    params = payload["params"]
    msg = EmailMessage()
    msg["Subject"] = params["subject"]
```

```
    msg["From"] = params["from"]
    msg["To"] = params["to"]
    msg.set_content(params["body"])
    for att in params.get("attachments", []):
        data = base64.b64decode(att["data"])
        msg.add_attachment(data, maintype="application",
subtype="pdf", filename=att["filename"])
    try:
        with smtplib.SMTP("smtp.example.com", 587) as smtp:
            smtp.starttls()
            smtp.login(os.getenv("SMTP_USER"),
os.getenv("SMTP_PASS"))
            smtp.send_message(msg)
    except Exception as e:
        raise HTTPException(status_code=502, detail=str(e))
    return
{"jsonrpc":"2.0","result":{"status":"sent"},"id":payload["id"
]}
```

With your manifest enforcing fields like `to`, `subject`, `body`, and an optional `attachments` array of Base64-encoded files, you ensure the agent can only send well-formed emails.

Together, these three tools—Data Reader, Chart Maker, and Email Sender—form the backbone of an automated reporting pipeline. By implementing each following the official Python documentation, validating inputs and outputs against your manifest schemas, and packaging them behind a single `/jsonrpc` endpoint, you give your Claude and GPT agents powerful, reliable primitives they can orchestrate to generate, visualize, and distribute business intelligence with a single prompt.

14.3 Exporting Markdown & PDF Reports

Once your agent has drafted its business report in Markdown—complete with headers, bullet points, tables, and embedded chart images—you need a reliable way to convert that Markdown into a polished, portable PDF. In this section, you'll build a two-step export pipeline following the exact patterns in the official Python `markdown` and `pdfkit` examples: first rendering Markdown to HTML with proper extensions, then feeding that HTML into `wkhtmltopdf` via `pdfkit` to produce a final report.pdf.

Begin by writing your agent's output to a `.md` file. In your orchestration code, after the **Draft Writer** agent returns its `report` string, save it:

```
report_md = response["report"]  # Markdown from GPT-4 or
Claude
md_path = "/tmp/business_report.md"
with open(md_path, "w", encoding="utf-8") as f:
    f.write(report_md)
```

Next, install the required libraries. As documented in the official `pdfkit` quickstart, you need both the Python package and the `wkhtmltopdf` binary:

```
pip install markdown pdfkit
sudo apt install wkhtmltopdf
```

With those in place, create a helper function—mirroring the official examples—that reads your Markdown file, converts it to HTML, wraps it in a simple template, and writes out the PDF:

```
import markdown
import pdfkit
import os

def export_markdown_to_pdf(md_file: str, pdf_file: str):
    # Step 1: Convert Markdown to HTML, enabling tables and
fenced code blocks
    with open(md_file, "r", encoding="utf-8") as f:
        md_text = f.read()
    html_body = markdown.markdown(md_text,
extensions=['tables','fenced_code'])

    # Step 2: Wrap the body in a minimal HTML document with
basic styling
    html = f"""
    <!DOCTYPE html>
    <html>
      <head>
        <meta charset="utf-8">
        <style>
          body {{ font-family: Arial, sans-serif; margin:
40px; }}
            h1, h2, h3 {{ color: #333; }}
```

```
            table {{ width: 100%; border-collapse: collapse;
margin-bottom: 20px; }}
            th, td {{ border: 1px solid #ccc; padding: 8px; }}
            pre {{ background: #f5f5f5; padding: 10px;
overflow: auto; }}
        </style>
    </head>
    <body>
        {html_body}
    </body>
</html>
    """


    # Step 3: Use pdfkit (wkhtmltopdf) to render HTML to PDF
    pdfkit.from_string(html, pdf_file)
    return pdf_file
```

To invoke this in your workflow, simply call:

```
md_path = "/tmp/business_report.md"
pdf_path = "/tmp/business_report.pdf"
exported = export_markdown_to_pdf(md_path, pdf_path)
print(f"Report exported to {exported}")
```

When you run this code, you'll see a complete PDF in
/tmp/business_report.pdf, styled consistently and preserving all
Markdown features—tables, code blocks, images, and more. Because
wkhtmltopdf leverages a real WebKit engine, your report renders exactly as
it would in a browser, giving you pixel-perfect control over margins, fonts,
and page breaks.

This two-step export process—Markdown→HTML→PDF—not only aligns
with the official markdown and pdfkit examples, but also integrates
seamlessly into your MCP agent. After the **Report Compiler** agent finishes
its draft, you call export_markdown_to_pdf and then use your **Email
Sender** tool (Chapter 14.2) to distribute the PDF to stakeholders. By the end
of this section, you'll have a fully automated pipeline that goes from data
ingestion to final PDF delivery, with each step backed by robust, battle-
tested Python libraries.

171

14.4 Triggering via Webhook & Scheduler

In production environments, business reports must run on demand—triggered by user actions via webhooks—and on a fixed schedule, such as weekly at market close. By combining a simple webhook endpoint with a cron scheduler, you can automate your Claude + GPT reporting pipeline end-to-end. In this section, you'll implement both triggers using FastAPI for the webhook and Linux cron for scheduling, following patterns from the official FastAPI and n8n examples to ensure secure, reliable invocation.

Begin by adding a `/trigger-report` endpoint in your FastAPI server. This lightweight webhook receives a POST with JSON parameters (for example, `reportType` and `recipients`) and enqueues an asynchronous background task to run your business report workflow:

```python
from fastapi import FastAPI, BackgroundTasks, Request,
HTTPException

app = FastAPI()

async def run_report_job(params: dict):
    # Orchestrate the agent: call Claude Research Agent or
Business Report Agent
    report = await
generate_business_report(params["reportType"])
    # Export and email
    pdf_path = export_markdown_to_pdf(report["markdown"],
"/tmp/report.pdf")
    await send_email(
        to=params["recipients"],
        subject=f"{params['reportType']} Report",
        body="Please find the attached report.",
        attachment_path=pdf_path
    )

@app.post("/trigger-report")
async def trigger_report(req: Request, bg: BackgroundTasks):
    payload = await req.json()
    if "reportType" not in payload or "recipients" not in
payload:
```

```
        raise HTTPException(status_code=400, detail="Missing
reportType or recipients")
    bg.add_task(run_report_job, payload)
    return {"status":"accepted","message":"Report job
enqueued"}
```

Deploy this endpoint to your cloud service (Render, Fly.io, etc.). Any external system—CI pipeline, dashboard button, or third-party app—can trigger a fresh report by POSTing:

```
curl -X POST https://your-app.com/trigger-report \
  -H "Content-Type: application/json" \
  -d '{"reportType":"Q2
Sales","recipients":["ceo@example.com"]}'
```

Next, automate scheduled runs using a Linux cron job that invokes this same webhook. On your server's console (or in your Docker container), run `crontab -e` and add:

```
0 18 * * Fri curl -X POST https://your-app.com/trigger-report
\
  -H "Content-Type: application/json" \
  -d '{"reportType":"Weekly
Business","recipients":["team@company.com"]}'
```

This cron line fires every Friday at 18:00 (market close), POSTing to `/trigger-report` and launching the background report job without manual intervention.

For environments that prefer no-code orchestration, you can achieve similar behavior in n8n by creating a workflow with a **Webhook** trigger node and a **HTTP Request** node. Configure the Webhook node to accept POST at `/n8n-webhook/report`, then add a Set node to map incoming JSON to the `reportType` and `recipients` fields, and finally invoke your local `/trigger-report` endpoint via the HTTP Request node. Use n8n's **Cron** node to schedule the workflow instead of system cron, setting it to run weekly on Fridays at 18:00.

By the end of this section, you'll have both push-button and scheduled automation for your report generator—leveraging FastAPI's background tasks and cron's familiar syntax or n8n's visual triggers—ensuring that your business intelligence is delivered exactly when and how stakeholders expect.

Chapter 15 | Customer Support Agent

15.1 Intake from File or API

The first critical step in any customer support agent is intake—standardizing incoming tickets so downstream logic can operate on a known structure. Whether tickets arrive as uploaded JSON files, CSV exports, or via a live webhook from your helpdesk API, your agent must normalize them into the same schema. In this section, you'll implement an MCP tool called `ingest_ticket` that reads a local `support_ticket.json` or calls a remote ticketing API endpoint, then returns a validated, uniform ticket object. Following the official FastAPI and JSON-RPC patterns, you'll see how simple it is to handle both file-based and HTTP-based intake with one tool definition.

Start by defining `ingest_ticket` in your `tool_manifest.json`. Its schema requires either a `path` parameter (for files) or a single `ticket_id` (for API fetch), and its output schema describes the unified ticket fields your agent expects:

```
{
  "name": "ingest_ticket",
  "description": "Loads a support ticket from a JSON file or
fetches it via API, returning a standardized ticket object.",
  "input_schema": {
    "type": "object",
    "properties": {
      "path":      { "type": "string" },
      "ticket_id": { "type": "string" }
    },
    "oneOf": [
      { "required": ["path"] },
      { "required": ["ticket_id"] }
    ],
    "additionalProperties": false
  },
  "output_schema": {
    "type": "object",
```

```
    "properties": {
      "ticket_id":          { "type": "string" },
      "customer_email": { "type": "string" },
      "subject":            { "type": "string" },
      "description":        { "type": "string" },
      "priority":           { "type": "string" },
      "timestamp":          { "type": "string", "format": "date-
time" }
    },
    "required":
["ticket_id","customer_email","subject","description","priori
ty","timestamp"]
  }
}
```

With the manifest in place, implement the FastAPI handler in
`handlers/ingest_ticket.py`. Use Python's file I/O to load local JSON
when `path` is provided, and `httpx` to call a helpdesk API when `ticket_id`
is given—mirroring examples from official FastAPI and HTTP clients:

```python
import os, json, httpx
from fastapi import HTTPException

HELPDESK_API_URL = os.getenv("HELPDESK_API_URL")
API_KEY          = os.getenv("HELPDESK_API_KEY")

async def ingest_ticket(params):
    if "path" in params:
        try:
            with open(params["path"], encoding="utf-8") as f:
                ticket = json.load(f)
        except FileNotFoundError:
            raise HTTPException(status_code=404,
detail="Ticket file not found")
    else:
        ticket_id = params["ticket_id"]
        headers = {"Authorization": f"Bearer {API_KEY}"}
        resp =
httpx.get(f"{HELPDESK_API_URL}/tickets/{ticket_id}",
headers=headers, timeout=5.0)
        if resp.status_code != 200:
            raise HTTPException(status_code=resp.status_code,
detail="Helpdesk API error")
        ticket = resp.json()
```

```
    # Normalize and validate structure
    try:
        standardized = {
            "ticket_id":       str(ticket["id"]),
            "customer_email": ticket["customer"]["email"],
            "subject":         ticket["subject"],
            "description":     ticket["description"],
            "priority":
ticket.get("priority","normal"),
            "timestamp":       ticket["created_at"]
        }
    except KeyError as e:
        raise HTTPException(status_code=422, detail=f"Missing
field in ticket data: {e}")

    return standardized
```

Integrate this handler into your JSON-RPC endpoint in `server.py` as shown in prior chapters. Then start the server:

```
uvicorn server:app --reload
```

Test local file intake via curl:

```
curl -X POST http://localhost:8000/jsonrpc \
  -H "Content-Type: application/json" \
  -d '{
    "jsonrpc":"2.0",
    "method":"ingest_ticket",
    "params":{"path":"./support_ticket.json"},
    "id":"intake-1"
  }'
```

And test API intake:

```
curl -X POST http://localhost:8000/jsonrpc \
  -H "Content-Type: application/json" \
  -d '{
    "jsonrpc":"2.0",
    "method":"ingest_ticket",
    "params":{"ticket_id":"A12498"},
    "id":"intake-2"
```

```
  }'
```

In both cases, you'll receive a consistent JSON object with `ticket_id`, `customer_email`, `subject`, `description`, `priority`, and `timestamp`. Back in the Claude Playground, set the manifest URL to your server and prompt:

```
Use ingest_ticket to load the new ticket, then draft an
initial customer acknowledgment email.
```

Claude emits the `tool_use` for `ingest_ticket`, your server returns the standardized ticket, and the agent proceeds. By the end of this section, you'll have a single MCP tool handling multiple intake modalities—file and API—delivering uniform context for your customer support workflows.

15.2 Retrieving Knowledge Articles

After ingesting a support ticket, the next crucial step is to ground your agent's response in authoritative, up-to-date knowledge—whether that lives in internal documentation, FAQ pages, or a curated knowledge base. In this section, you'll implement an MCP tool named `retrieve_kb_article` that queries your document store for the most relevant articles, following the official Anthropic RAG example. You'll see how to embed your knowledge search logic in a FastAPI handler, validate inputs against your manifest schema, and return precisely the snippets your agent needs to draft accurate, context-aware replies.

Begin by adding `retrieve_kb_article` to your `tool_manifest.json`. The input schema accepts a single `topic` string, while the output schema returns an array of objects, each containing `title`, `url`, and `excerpt`:

```
{
  "name": "retrieve_kb_article",
  "description": "Fetches the top matching knowledge-base
articles for a given topic.",
  "input_schema": {
    "type": "object",
    "properties": {
      "topic": { "type": "string", "description": "Keyword to
search in KB articles." }
    },
```

177

```
    "required": ["topic"],
    "additionalProperties": false
  },
  "output_schema": {
    "type": "array",
    "items": {
      "type": "object",
      "properties": {
        "title":   { "type": "string" },
        "url":     { "type": "string" },
        "excerpt": { "type": "string" }
      },
      "required": ["title","url","excerpt"]
    }
  }
}
```

With the manifest in place, implement the handler in
`handlers/retrieve_kb_article.py`. Drawing on Anthropic's official
vector-search example, you'll load your pre-indexed Chroma database on
startup and perform a similarity search at runtime:

```
from fastapi import HTTPException
from pydantic import BaseModel
from langchain.embeddings import OpenAIEmbeddings
from langchain.vectorstores import Chroma

# Initialize Chroma vector store once
embedding = OpenAIEmbeddings()
vectordb = Chroma(persist_directory="./kb_chroma",
embedding_function=embedding)

class KBParams(BaseModel):
    topic: str

async def retrieve_kb_article(params: KBParams):
    try:
        docs = vectordb.similarity_search(params.topic, k=3)
    except Exception as e:
        raise HTTPException(status_code=502, detail=f"Vector
DB error: {str(e)}")

    results = []
    for doc in docs:
```

```
        results.append({
            "title": doc.metadata.get("title", "Untitled"),
            "url": doc.metadata.get("source", ""),
            "excerpt": doc.page_content[:200]  # first 200
chars
        })
    return results
```

Here, we rely on the official `langchain` and `Chroma` patterns to index and
query your KB. Each returned `doc` includes `metadata` fields and
`page_content`; you map those into the required schema. By validating
`params.topic` against the manifest's input schema, you ensure only well-
formed requests proceed.

Start your tool server (`uvicorn server:app --reload`) and test the new
tool via curl:

```
curl -X POST http://localhost:8000/jsonrpc \
  -H "Content-Type: application/json" \
  -d '{
    "jsonrpc":"2.0",
    "method":"retrieve_kb_article",
    "params":{"topic":"password reset"},
    "id":"kb-1"
  }'
```

You'll receive a JSON array of up to three articles, each with a `title`, `url`,
and excerpt—exactly matching the manifest's `output_schema`.

Finally, in the Claude Playground, configure the manifest URL to point at
your local server and prompt:

```
A user cannot reset their password. Use retrieve_kb_article
to fetch relevant KB articles on password reset procedures,
then draft a clear troubleshooting response.
```

Claude emits a `tool_use` directive for `retrieve_kb_article`, your service
returns the array of articles, and the model generates a precise, citation-
backed reply. This seamlessly integrates your knowledge base into the
support workflow, ensuring customers receive accurate, contextually
relevant assistance without manually re-searching documentation.

15.3 Suggested Reply Generator

Once your agent has both the standardized ticket data and the most relevant knowledge-base excerpts, the next step is to draft a suggested reply that combines empathy with technical accuracy. In this section, you'll implement an MCP tool named `generate_reply` that takes a support ticket object and an array of KB articles, then calls Claude to produce a ready-to-send response. By following the official Anthropic chat-completion patterns, you'll see how to structure your prompt, handle the function output, and validate the final reply against your manifest schema.

Begin by declaring the tool in `tool_manifest.json`. Its `input_schema` requires both the `ticket` object (as defined in Section 15.1) and a `kb_results` array, while its `output_schema` expects a single `reply` string:

```
{
  "name": "generate_reply",
  "description": "Drafts a customer reply using the ticket
details and KB articles.",
  "input_schema": {
    "type": "object",
    "properties": {
      "ticket": {
        "type": "object",
        "properties": {
          "ticket_id":       { "type": "string" },
          "customer_email": { "type": "string" },
          "subject":         { "type": "string" },
          "description":     { "type": "string" },
          "priority":        { "type": "string" },
          "timestamp":       { "type": "string", "format":
"date-time" }
        },
        "required":
["ticket_id","customer_email","description"]
      },
      "kb_results": {
        "type": "array",
        "items": {
          "type": "object",
          "properties": {
```

```
              "title":    { "type": "string" },
              "url":      { "type": "string" },
              "excerpt": { "type": "string" }
            },
            "required": ["title","url","excerpt"]
          }
        }
      },
      "required": ["ticket","kb_results"],
      "additionalProperties": false
    },
    "output_schema": {
      "type": "object",
      "properties": {
        "reply": { "type": "string" }
      },
      "required": ["reply"]
    }
  }
}
```

With the manifest in place, implement the handler in
`handlers/generate_reply.py`. You'll mirror the Anthropic chat-
completion example: construct a system prompt that positions Claude as a
courteous support agent, feed the ticket and KB results as context, and
instruct Claude to output only the reply text. A minimal FastAPI handler
looks like this:

```
from fastapi import HTTPException
from anthropic import Anthropic, HUMAN_PROMPT, AI_PROMPT
from pydantic import BaseModel

client = Anthropic(api_key="YOUR_CLAUDE_KEY")

class GenerateReplyParams(BaseModel):
    ticket: dict
    kb_results: list[dict]

async def generate_reply(params: GenerateReplyParams):
    ticket = params.ticket
    kb = params.kb_results

    system_msg = (
        f"{HUMAN_PROMPT}"
        "You are a helpful customer support agent. "
```

```python
        "Using the ticket information and KB articles, draft
a concise, empathetic reply. "
        "Do not include any tool calls—return only the email
text. "
        f"{AI_PROMPT}"
    )

    user_msg = (
        f"Ticket #{ticket['ticket_id']} from
{ticket['customer_email']}:\n"
        f"Subject: {ticket['subject']}\n"
        f"Description: {ticket['description']}\n\n"
        "Relevant KB articles:\n"
    )
    for art in kb:
        user_msg += f"- {art['title']} ({art['url']}):
{art['excerpt']}\n"

    try:
        resp = client.completions.create(
            model="claude-3-opus",
            prompt=system_msg + user_msg,
            max_tokens_to_sample=300
        )
        reply_text = resp.completion.strip()
    except Exception as e:
        raise HTTPException(status_code=502, detail=str(e))

    return {"reply": reply_text}
```

Once you've added this handler to your JSON-RPC endpoint, start the server
(`uvicorn server:app --reload`) and test via curl:

```
curl -X POST http://localhost:8000/jsonrpc \
  -H "Content-Type:application/json" \
  -d '{
    "jsonrpc":"2.0",
    "method":"generate_reply",
    "params":{
      "ticket": {
        "ticket_id":"A12498",
        "customer_email":"jane@example.com",
        "subject":"Login issue",
```

```
      "description":"I cannot log in after resetting my
password.",
      "priority":"high",
      "timestamp":"2025-06-10T09:15:00Z"
    },
    "kb_results": [
      {
        "title":"Password Reset Guide",
        "url":"https://company.com/kb/password-reset",
        "excerpt":"After resetting your password, it may
take up to 5 minutes for changes to propagate."
      }
    ]
  },
  "id":"reply-1"
}'
```

You'll receive a JSON-RPC response with a single `"reply"` field containing a well-formed, empathetic email ready for review or automatic dispatch. By the end of this exercise, you'll have a robust suggested-reply generator—powered by structured prompts and validated schemas—that elevates your customer support agent from reactive to proactive, ensuring consistency, tone, and accuracy in every interaction.

15.4 Logging, Feedback & Chatbot Integration

In a production customer support agent, every interaction—prompt, tool invocation, and agent reply—must be traceable and improvable. Implementing structured logging and user feedback loops lets you monitor performance, tune prompts, and integrate seamlessly into chat interfaces like Slack or Microsoft Teams. In this section, you'll extend your FastAPI JSON-RPC server to emit rich, contextual logs for each `generate_reply` call, capture feedback scores via a secondary endpoint, and wire the entire workflow into a Slack chatbot using Block Kit—following the official Slack and FastAPI integration examples.

Begin by configuring your FastAPI server to log each request and response with a unique ticket identifier. At the top of `server.py`, set up a JSON logger:

```
import logging, sys, json
logging.basicConfig(stream=sys.stdout, level=logging.INFO,
format='%(message)s')
logger = logging.getLogger("support_agent")
```

Wrap your JSON-RPC handler so it logs the incoming `method`, `params["ticket"]["ticket_id"]`, and the resulting `reply`:

```
@app.post("/jsonrpc")
async def handle_rpc(req: Request):
    payload = await req.json()
    method = payload["method"]
    request_id = payload.get("id")
    ticket_id = payload["params"]["ticket"]["ticket_id"]
    logger.info(json.dumps({
        "event": "request_received",
        "method": method,
        "ticket_id": ticket_id,
        "request_id": request_id
    }))
    # ... invoke handler ...
    result = await generate_reply(payload["params"])
    logger.info(json.dumps({
        "event": "reply_generated",
        "ticket_id": ticket_id,
        "reply": result["reply"]
    }))
    return {"jsonrpc":"2.0","result":result,"id":request_id}
```

Next, implement a feedback endpoint that agents or end-users can call after reviewing a draft. Following FastAPI's request-body pattern, add:

```
from pydantic import BaseModel

class Feedback(BaseModel):
    ticket_id: str
    rating: int  # 1-5 scale
    comments: str | None = None

@app.post("/feedback")
async def submit_feedback(feedback: Feedback):
    logger.info(json.dumps({
        "event": "feedback_received",
```

184

```
        "ticket_id": feedback.ticket_id,
        "rating": feedback.rating,
        "comments": feedback.comments
    }))
    return {"status":"ok"}
```

This endpoint writes structured feedback logs, enabling later analysis of agent performance and prompt effectiveness.

Finally, integrate your agent into Slack so support staff can review, edit, and approve replies within their existing chat flow. Using the official Slack Bolt framework, mount a command—/reply_ticket—that invokes your MCP server, presents the draft in a Block Kit message, and attaches interactive buttons for "Send," "Edit," and "👍/👎" feedback:

```
from slack_bolt import App
import requests

slack = App(token=os.getenv("SLACK_BOT_TOKEN"),
signing_secret=os.getenv("SLACK_SIGNING_SECRET"))

@slack.command("/reply_ticket")
def handle_reply(ack, body, client):
    ack()
    ticket_id = body["text"].strip()
    # Call MCP ingest and reply generation
    ingest_resp = requests.post("https://your-
server/jsonrpc", json={…})
    draft = ingest_resp.json()["result"]["reply"]
    # Post draft with buttons
    client.chat_postMessage(
        channel=body["channel_id"],
        blocks=[

{"type":"section","text":{"type":"mrkdwn","text":f"*Draft
Reply for {ticket_id}:*\n{draft}"}},
            {"type":"actions","elements":[

{"type":"button","text":{"type":"plain_text","text":"Send"},"
value":ticket_id,"action_id":"send_reply"},

{"type":"button","text":{"type":"plain_text","text":"👍"},"val
ue":f"{ticket_id}|1","action_id":"feedback"},
```

```
{"type":"button","text":{"type":"plain_text","text":"🏷"},"val
ue":f"{ticket_id}|0","action_id":"feedback"}
            ]}
        ]
    )
```

Handle button clicks to either POST the reply via your email tool or call the
/feedback endpoint:

```
@slack.action("send_reply")
def send_reply(ack, body):
    ack()
    ticket_id = body["actions"][0]["value"]
    # invoke email sender, then log
    requests.post("https://your-server/send_email", json={…})

logger.info(json.dumps({"event":"reply_sent","ticket_id":tick
et_id}))

@slack.action("feedback")
def handle_feedback(ack, body):
    ack()
    ticket_id, score = body["actions"][0]["value"].split("|")
    requests.post("https://your-server/feedback",
json={"ticket_id":ticket_id,"rating":int(score)})
```

With this integration, your support staff see the agent's drafts, provide
immediate feedback, and trigger final dispatch—all within Slack. Behind the
scenes, your FastAPI server logs each event consistently, feeding into
dashboards or analytics pipelines that measure agent accuracy and user
satisfaction.

By combining structured logging, a dedicated feedback endpoint, and a Slack
chatbot integration—each modeled on official documentation—you create a
closed-loop support system where context-aware agents draft replies,
humans review and rate them, and operations teams monitor performance in
real time. This pattern elevates your MCP-based customer support agents
from isolated proof-of-concepts to seamless, team-integrated production
tools.

Chapter 16 | Personal Productivity Agent

16.1 Day Planner & Task Categorizer

A personal productivity agent transforms lists of unstructured tasks into an actionable day plan, assigning priorities and time slots so that you—and your team—can hit the ground running each morning. Building such an agent with Claude involves three key capabilities: parsing natural-language to-do lists, categorizing tasks by effort or domain, and slotting them into available calendar windows. In this section, you'll implement a "day_planner" tool and a "task_categorizer" tool—each declared in your MCP manifest and wired into FastAPI handlers—then orchestrate them in a single Claude session to produce a ready-to-use schedule.

First, define your tools in `tool_manifest.json`. The **"task_categorizer"** accepts an array of free-form task descriptions and returns an array of objects { name, category, priority }. The **"day_planner"** takes those categorized tasks along with a JSON object describing "working_hours" and "existing_events," and returns a list of scheduled slots { name, start, end }. Your manifest entries mirror the official Anthropic examples for similar scheduling tools:

```
{
  "tools": [
    {
      "name": "task_categorizer",
      "description": "Classifies tasks into domains and
assigns a priority level.",
      "input_schema": {
        "type":"object",
        "properties":{
          "tasks":{"type":"array","items":{"type":"string"}}
        },
        "required":["tasks"]
      },
      "output_schema":{
        "type":"array",
        "items":{
```

187

```
            "type":"object",
            "properties":{
              "name":{"type":"string"},
              "category":{"type":"string"},

"priority":{"type":"string","enum":["high","medium","low"]}
            },
            "required":["name","category","priority"]
          }
      }
    },
    {
      "name": "day_planner",
      "description": "Schedules categorized tasks into
available calendar slots.",
      "input_schema":{
        "type":"object",
        "properties":{

"tasks":{"type":"array","items":{"$ref":"#/tools/0/output_sch
ema/items"}},
          "working_hours":{
            "type":"object",
            "properties":{
              "start":{"type":"string","format":"time"},
              "end":{"type":"string","format":"time"}
            },
            "required":["start","end"]
          },
          "existing_events":{
            "type":"array",
            "items":{
              "type":"object",
              "properties":{
                "start":{"type":"string","format":"date-
time"},
                "end":{"type":"string","format":"date-time"}
              },
              "required":["start","end"]
            }
          }
        },
        "required":["tasks","working_hours"]
      },
```

```
      "output_schema":{
        "type":"array",
        "items":{
          "type":"object",
          "properties":{
            "name":{"type":"string"},
            "start":{"type":"string","format":"date-time"},
            "end":{"type":"string","format":"date-time"}
          },
          "required":["name","start","end"]
        }
      }
    }
  ]
}
```

With your manifest ready, implement `handlers/task_categorizer.py`
using Claude's official few-shot recipe for classification: load the Anthropic
client, send a prompt listing example tasks and their categories, then parse
Claude's JSON response:

```python
from anthropic import Anthropic, HUMAN_PROMPT, AI_PROMPT
import json

client = Anthropic(api_key="YOUR_CLAUDE_KEY")

async def task_categorizer(params):
    tasks = params["tasks"]
    examples = [
        {"task":"Write Q2
report","category":"work","priority":"high"},
        {"task":"Buy
groceries","category":"personal","priority":"medium"}
    ]
    prompt = f"{HUMAN_PROMPT}Classify each task into category
and priority. Respond in JSON array of
{{name,category,priority}}.{AI_PROMPT}"
    for ex in examples:
        prompt += f"\n\nTask: {ex['task']}\nCategory:
{ex['category']}\nPriority: {ex['priority']}"
    for t in tasks:
        prompt += f"\n\nTask: {t}"
    resp = client.completions.create(model="claude-3-opus",
prompt=prompt, max_tokens_to_sample=300)
```

```
    return json.loads(resp.completion)
```

Next, in `handlers/day_planner.py`, use Python's `datetime` library—following the official datetime tutorials—to allocate each task into open slots. Begin by parsing working hours and existing events, then iterate through tasks, assigning them in order of priority to the first available window, respecting event conflicts:

```python
from datetime import datetime, timedelta
from fastapi import HTTPException

async def day_planner(params):
    tasks = params["tasks"]
    wh = params["working_hours"]
    events = params.get("existing_events", [])
    start = datetime.fromisoformat(wh["start"])
    end   = datetime.fromisoformat(wh["end"])

    scheduled = []
    cursor = start
    for t in sorted(tasks, key=lambda x:
{"high":0,"medium":1,"low":2}[x["priority"]]):
        duration = timedelta(hours=1)   # assume 1h per task
        # advance cursor past events
        for ev in events:
            ev_start = datetime.fromisoformat(ev["start"])
            ev_end   = datetime.fromisoformat(ev["end"])
            if cursor >= ev_start and cursor < ev_end:
                cursor = ev_end
        if cursor + duration > end:
            raise HTTPException(status_code=422, detail="Not
enough time to schedule tasks")
        scheduled.append({
            "name": t["name"],
            "start": cursor.isoformat(),
            "end":   (cursor+duration).isoformat()
        })
        cursor += duration
    return scheduled
```

Finally, orchestrate both tools in a Claude session—first calling `task_categorizer`, then feeding its output into `day_planner` along with your working hours and existing calendar events. Claude's `tool_use` directives will drive each step, and your shared MCP client handles the JSON-RPC calls seamlessly. By following the official examples to the letter—leveraging few-shot classification, datetime parsing best practices, and manifest-driven validation—you create a personal productivity agent that turns a simple to-do list into a structured, prioritized, and conflict-aware daily schedule.

16.2 Writing Summaries & Reminders to File

Writing summaries and reminders to disk transforms ephemeral conversation into a persistent record your productivity agent and users can revisit at any time. In this section, you'll implement an MCP tool named `write_to_file` that accepts a structured summary and reminder list, serializes them to a Markdown file, and returns the file path for downstream steps such as email attachments. Following the official Python file-I/O patterns, you'll validate inputs against your manifest's schema, handle filesystem errors gracefully, and ensure your agent can rely on durable outputs rather than transient chat.

Begin by declaring `write_to_file` in your `tool_manifest.json` alongside your other tools:

```
{
  "name": "write_to_file",
  "description": "Appends a daily summary and reminders to a
Markdown log file.",
  "input_schema": {
    "type": "object",
    "properties": {
      "date":      { "type": "string", "format": "date" },
      "summary":   { "type": "string" },
      "reminders": {
        "type": "array",
        "items": { "type": "string" }
      }
    },
    "required": ["date","summary","reminders"],
    "additionalProperties": false
  },
  "output_schema": {
    "type": "object",
    "properties": {
```

```
        "file_path": { "type": "string" }
    },
    "required": ["file_path"]
  }
}
```
With the manifest in place, implement the handler in
`handlers/write_to_file.py`:
```python
import os
from fastapi import HTTPException

async def write_to_file(params):
    date = params["date"]
    summary = params["summary"].strip()
    reminders = params["reminders"]

    # Construct the Markdown content
    md = f"# Daily Summary — {date}\n\n"
    md += "## Summary\n\n"
    md += summary + "\n\n"
    md += "## Reminders\n\n"
    for r in reminders:
        md += f"- {r}\n"
    md += "\n---\n\n"

    # Ensure the logs directory exists
    logs_dir = "./logs"
    os.makedirs(logs_dir, exist_ok=True)

    file_path = os.path.join(logs_dir, f"daily_{date}.md")
    try:
        # Append if exists, otherwise create
        with open(file_path, "a", encoding="utf-8") as f:
            f.write(md)
    except OSError as e:
        raise HTTPException(status_code=500, detail=f"File
write error: {e.strerror}")

    return {"file_path": file_path}
```

Here you follow the official Python I/O tutorial: creating directories with
`os.makedirs`, opening files in append mode, and catching `OSError` to return
a clear JSON-RPC error if the filesystem is read-only or full.

Start your server (`uvicorn server:app --reload`) and test the tool locally:

192

```
curl -X POST http://127.0.0.1:8000/jsonrpc \
  -H "Content-Type: application/json" \
  -d '{
    "jsonrpc":"2.0",
    "method":"write_to_file",
    "params":{
      "date":"2025-06-10",
      "summary":"Completed the Q3 financial model and
reviewed team OKRs.",
      "reminders":["Follow up on vendor invoice","Plan next
sprint backlog","Schedule 1:1 with manager"]
    },
    "id":"log-1"
  }'
```

You'll receive:

```
{"jsonrpc":"2.0","result":{"file_path":"./logs/daily_2025-06-
10.md"},"id":"log-1"}
```

Inspect `./logs/daily_2025-06-10.md` to see:

```
# Daily Summary — 2025-06-10

## Summary

Completed the Q3 financial model and reviewed team OKRs.

## Reminders

- Follow up on vendor invoice
- Plan next sprint backlog
- Schedule 1:1 with manager

---
```

Finally, in your Claude orchestration, after generating summary and reminders, call `write_to_file` so every agent session produces a durable record. This persistent log can feed into your calendar tool, email sender, or long-term memory, giving your productivity agent the continuity and recall needed for multi-day planning. By following the official file-I/O patterns step by step, you ensure robustness, clear error reporting, and instantly usable output files for any downstream automation.

16.3 Calendar Scheduling & Goal Tracking

Linking your task planner to a real calendar and tracking goal completion transforms a static schedule into a living roadmap you—and your agent—can revisit, update, and analyze over time. In this section, you'll implement two MCP tools—`create_calendar_event` and `track_goal`—that respectively book time slots in Google Calendar and record goal status in a JSON-backed datastore. You'll follow the official Google Calendar quickstart and Python file-I/O examples to ensure your implementation matches production best practices.

Begin by adding both tools to your `tool_manifest.json`. The `create_calendar_event` tool accepts `summary`, an ISO-8601 `start` and `end` time, and an optional `timeZone`; the `track_goal` tool takes a `goal_id` and a `status` string:

```
{
  "tools": [
    {
      "name": "create_calendar_event",
      "description": "Creates an event on the user's primary
Google Calendar.",
      "input_schema": {
        "type": "object",
        "properties": {
          "summary":    { "type": "string" },
          "start":      { "type": "string", "format": "date-
time" },
          "end":        { "type": "string", "format": "date-
time" },
          "timeZone":   { "type": "string" }
        },
        "required": ["summary","start","end"]
      },
      "output_schema": {
        "type": "object",
        "properties": {
          "event_id":   { "type": "string" }
        },
        "required": ["event_id"]
      }
```

```
      },
      {
        "name": "track_goal",
        "description": "Records the status of a user goal in
persistent storage.",
        "input_schema": {
          "type": "object",
          "properties": {
            "goal_id": { "type": "string" },
            "status": { "type": "string", "enum":
["planned","in_progress","completed"] }
          },
          "required": ["goal_id","status"]
        },
        "output_schema": {
          "type": "object",
          "properties": {
            "recorded_at": { "type": "string", "format": "date-
time" }
          },
          "required": ["recorded_at"]
        }
      }
    ]
}
```

With your manifest ready, implement the **Google Calendar** event creator in `handlers/create_calendar_event.py`. Following the official Python quickstart, you first set up OAuth 2.0 credentials and the Calendar API client:

```
from google.oauth2 import service_account
from googleapiclient.discovery import build
from datetime import datetime
import os
from fastapi import HTTPException

SCOPES = ['https://www.googleapis.com/auth/calendar.events']
SERVICE_ACCOUNT_FILE = os.getenv("GOOGLE_CREDENTIALS_PATH")
credentials =
service_account.Credentials.from_service_account_file(
    SERVICE_ACCOUNT_FILE, scopes=SCOPES
)
service = build('calendar', 'v3', credentials=credentials)
```

```
async def create_calendar_event(params):
    event_body = {
        'summary': params['summary'],
        'start': {'dateTime': params['start'], 'timeZone':
params.get('timeZone','UTC')},
        'end':   {'dateTime': params['end'],   'timeZone':
params.get('timeZone','UTC')}
    }
    try:
        event = service.events().insert(calendarId='primary',
body=event_body).execute()
    except Exception as e:
        raise HTTPException(status_code=502,
detail=f"Calendar API error: {e}")
    return {'event_id': event.get('id')}
```

Next, create the **Goal Tracker** in `handlers/track_goal.py`. You'll store each record in a local JSON file—mirroring the official Python JSON example—and timestamp it:

```
import json
from datetime import datetime
from fastapi import HTTPException

GOALS_FILE = './data/goals.json'

async def track_goal(params):
    record = {
        'goal_id': params['goal_id'],
        'status':  params['status'],
        'recorded_at': datetime.utcnow().isoformat() + 'Z'
    }
    try:
        try:
            with open(GOALS_FILE, 'r', encoding='utf-8') as
f:
                data = json.load(f)
        except FileNotFoundError:
            data = []
        data.append(record)
        with open(GOALS_FILE, 'w', encoding='utf-8') as f:
            json.dump(data, f, indent=2)
    except Exception as e:
```

```
        raise HTTPException(status_code=500, detail=f"Goal
tracking error: {e}")
    return {'recorded_at': record['recorded_at']}
```

With handlers implemented, start your server (`uvicorn server:app --reload`) and test both tools via curl:

```
curl -X POST http://localhost:8000/jsonrpc -H "Content-
Type:application/json" -d '{
  "jsonrpc":"2.0","method":"create_calendar_event",
  "params":{"summary":"Team Sync","start":"2025-06-
11T14:00:00Z","end":"2025-06-11T15:00:00Z","timeZone":"UTC"},
  "id":"cal-1"
}'
curl -X POST http://localhost:8000/jsonrpc -H "Content-
Type:application/json" -d '{
  "jsonrpc":"2.0","method":"track_goal",
  "params":{"goal_id":"goal-123","status":"planned"},
  "id":"track-1"
}'
```

Finally, orchestrate these calls in your productivity agent: after Claude proposes a plan slot, you call `create_calendar_event` to book each time block, then call `track_goal` with status `"planned"` or `"completed"` as the day progresses. By the end of this section, you'll have live calendar integrations and a persistent goal log—complete with timestamps—giving your personal productivity agent the structure and accountability required for real-world use.

16.4 Self-Evaluation & Auto-Feedback Loops

Every agent—even one built for personal productivity—benefits from a built-in mechanism to reflect on its own performance and improve over time. Self-evaluation closes the loop: after your agent executes a plan, it analyzes successes and failures, then adjusts future behavior automatically. In this section, you'll add a new MCP tool, `evaluate_goals`, that reads your persisted goal log, invokes Claude to generate feedback on completion rates, and writes that feedback back into your system. You'll follow the official Anthropic few-shot evaluation pattern, implement the FastAPI handler, and

197

wire it into your workflow so every day's performance informs tomorrow's plan.

Begin by extending your manifest (`tool_manifest.json`) with the `evaluate_goals` entry. Its input schema expects a `session_id` so it can load the day's goals, and its output schema returns an array of objects with `goal_id`, `status`, and `feedback`:

```json
{
  "name": "evaluate_goals",
  "description": "Reads all goals for a session and uses
Claude to generate constructive feedback for each.",
  "input_schema": {
    "type": "object",
    "properties": {
      "session_id": { "type": "string" }
    },
    "required": ["session_id"],
    "additionalProperties": false
  },
  "output_schema": {
    "type": "array",
    "items": {
      "type": "object",
      "properties": {
        "goal_id": { "type": "string" },
        "status":  { "type": "string" },
        "feedback": { "type": "string" }
      },
      "required": ["goal_id","status","feedback"]
    }
  }
}
```

Next, implement the handler in `handlers/evaluate_goals.py`, drawing on the official Anthropic evaluation examples. You load your JSON goal log (created by `track_goal`), construct a few-shot prompt with examples of good and poor completion, and ask Claude to provide feedback for each goal:

```python
import json
from fastapi import HTTPException
from anthropic import Anthropic, HUMAN_PROMPT, AI_PROMPT
```

198

```python
client = Anthropic(api_key="YOUR_CLAUDE_KEY")
GOALS_FILE = "./data/goals.json"

async def evaluate_goals(params):
    session = params["session_id"]
    # Load all recorded goals for this session
    try:
        with open(GOALS_FILE, encoding="utf-8") as f:
            all_goals = json.load(f)
    except FileNotFoundError:
        raise HTTPException(status_code=404, detail="No goals
found")

    # Filter goals for this session
    session_goals = [g for g in all_goals if
g.get("session_id")==session]
    if not session_goals:
        raise HTTPException(status_code=404, detail="No goals
for session")

    # Build few-shot prompt
    prompt = f"{HUMAN_PROMPT}Provide feedback on each goal's
completion. For goals marked 'completed', reinforce success;
for others, suggest improvements. Return JSON array.\n\n"
    # Example
    prompt += (
        "Example:\n"
        "Goal ID: g1, Status: completed → Feedback:
"Excellent work finishing this on time. Continue this
pace."\n"
        "Goal ID: g2, Status: planned   → Feedback: "Consider
breaking this into smaller tasks."\n\n"
    )
    # Add user data
    for g in session_goals:
        prompt += f"Goal ID: {g['goal_id']}, Status:
{g['status']}\n"
    prompt += AI_PROMPT

    resp = client.completions.create(
        model="claude-3-opus",
        prompt=prompt,
        max_tokens_to_sample=200
```

```
    )
    # Parse Claude's JSON output
    try:
        feedback_list = json.loads(resp.completion)
    except json.JSONDecodeError as e:
        raise HTTPException(status_code=500, detail="Invalid
JSON from Claude")

    return feedback_list
```

With this tool in place, you extend your daily workflow so that, after the planner and tracker run, the agent calls `evaluate_goals`. Its output appends to a feedback log or even updates the goal statuses for the next iteration. In practice, you trigger this in your orchestration script:

```
# After scheduling and tracking…
feedback = await call_tool("evaluate_goals", {"session_id":
session_id})
# Persist or present feedback as needed
```

This auto-feedback loop ensures your productivity agent not only plans and schedules, but also learns from every day—highlighting wins, diagnosing stalls, and suggesting corrective actions. By following the official evaluation patterns and schema-driven integration, you create a truly adaptive agent that grows more effective with each cycle.

Part VII | QA, Security & Production Readiness

Chapter 1 7| Evaluation & Observability

17.1 Simulating Prompt & Tool Flows

Simulating your agent's prompt and tool flows in a local sandbox is the fastest way to catch integration bugs before they reach users. Rather than waiting for a full end-to-end Claude session, you can replay the exact JSON-RPC messages your model emits, mock tool responses, and verify that your orchestration logic handles every branch correctly. This approach mirrors the official Anthropic testing recommendations and gives you confidence that your workflows behave identically in production.

Imagine you have an agent that, when asked "Summarize the facts of document X," issues a `tool_use` for `read_file`, then a `tool_use` for `summarize_text`. To simulate this flow, extract the two JSON-RPC calls and hard-code mock responses in a simple Python script:

```python
# simulate_flow.py

import json

# Step 1: Agent issues read_file call
read_request = {
    "jsonrpc": "2.0",
    "method": "read_file",
    "params": {"path": "docs/report.pdf"},
    "id": "1"
}
print("REQUEST 1 →", json.dumps(read_request, indent=2))

# Mock the tool response exactly as your server would return
read_response = {
    "jsonrpc": "2.0",
    "result": {"content": "Annual report shows 15%
growth..."},
    "id": "1"
}
```

```
print("MOCK RESPONSE 1 →", json.dumps(read_response,
indent=2))


# Step 2: Agent issues summarize_text call with the content
from response 1
summ_request = {
    "jsonrpc": "2.0",
    "method": "summarize_text",
    "params": {"text": read_response["result"]["content"]},
    "id": "2"
}
print("REQUEST 2 →", json.dumps(summ_request, indent=2))


# Mock the summarizer's JSON output
summ_response = {
    "jsonrpc": "2.0",
    "result": {"summary": "Report indicates a 15% increase in
annual growth."},
    "id": "2"
}
print("MOCK RESPONSE 2 →", json.dumps(summ_response,
indent=2))


# Validate final result
final_summary = summ_response["result"]["summary"]
print("\nFINAL SUMMARY →", final_summary)
```

Running this script reproduces exactly how your agent and tools interact, allowing you to verify:

1. That the second request uses the `content` field from the first response without manual copy-paste.
2. That your JSON-RPC envelopes—`method`, `params`, and `id`—match the manifest's schemas.
3. That your orchestration code correctly parses `mock_responses` and proceeds to the final summary step.

For more sophisticated scenarios—branching logic, error retries, or multi-tool sequences—you can extend this pattern. For example, to simulate an error in the `summarize_text` step, change the mock response to:

```
summ_response = {
  "jsonrpc":"2.0",
```

```
  "error":{"code":-32000,"message":"Timeout while
summarizing."},
  "id":"2"
}
```

and verify that your orchestration code catches this error, logs it, and either retries or falls back to a default behavior. By automating these simulations, you create a lightweight test suite that ensures every possible tool-call path is exercised under controlled conditions.

Ultimately, simulating prompt and tool flows demystifies the agent's internal decision-making and highlights mismatches between manifest, handler logic, and orchestration code. This practice—directly inspired by the official FastAPI and Anthropic examples—becomes the cornerstone of a dependable CI pipeline, catching integration bugs early and guaranteeing that your context-aware agents perform exactly as intended in production.

17.2 Streaming Logs & Output Debugging

Streaming responses from Claude give you real-time insight into the agent's reasoning and tool-selection process, making it far easier to diagnose issues than waiting for a full completion. In this section, you'll instrument your client and server to log every partial chunk, detect tool-call directives mid-stream, and capture malformed JSON before it causes downstream failures—precisely as demonstrated in the official Anthropic streaming example.

Start on the client side. When you enable streaming in the Anthropic SDK, you receive an asynchronous generator yielding `chunk` objects. Wrap that generator to log each piece as it arrives:

```
from anthropic import Anthropic, HUMAN_PROMPT, AI_PROMPT
import logging, asyncio

logging.basicConfig(level=logging.DEBUG)
logger = logging.getLogger("stream_debug")

client = Anthropic(api_key="…")

async def debug_stream(prompt: str):
    stream = await client.completions.create(
```

```
        model="claude-3-opus",
        prompt=f"{HUMAN_PROMPT}{prompt}{AI_PROMPT}",
        max_tokens_to_sample=300,
        stream=True
    )
    buffer = ""
    async for chunk in stream:
        token = chunk.completion
        buffer += token
        logger.debug(f"STREAM TOKEN: {repr(token)}")
        # Detect and log tool_use directives immediately
        if '"tool_use"' in buffer:
            start = buffer.index('"tool_use"')
            snippet = buffer[start:start+200]
            logger.info(f"Detected tool_use directive:
{snippet}")
        # Optionally, attempt to parse JSON when complete
        if buffer.strip().endswith("}"):
            try:
                parsed = json.loads(buffer)
                logger.debug(f"Parsed JSON: {parsed}")
                buffer = ""  # clear for next JSON block
            except json.JSONDecodeError:
                logger.debug("Incomplete JSON, waiting for
more tokens")
```

When you run `debug_stream("Your prompt here")`, you'll see each token printed, the moment a `tool_use` directive appears, and any successful JSON parses. This instantaneous feedback pinpoints exactly where your agent's protocol messages deviate from your manifest.

On the server side, configure FastAPI to log raw request bodies and JSON-RPC responses for debugging. Add a middleware similar to the official FastAPI example:

```
from starlette.middleware.base import BaseHTTPMiddleware

class LogMiddleware(BaseHTTPMiddleware):
    async def dispatch(self, request, call_next):
        body = await request.body()
        logger.debug(f"RAW REQUEST: {body.decode()}")
        response = await call_next(request)
        resp_body = b"".join([chunk async for chunk in
response.body_iterator])
```

```
        logger.debug(f"RAW RESPONSE: {resp_body.decode()}")
        return Response(content=resp_body,
status_code=response.status_code,
headers=dict(response.headers))


app.add_middleware(LogMiddleware)
```

This middleware prints every incoming JSON-RPC envelope and every response your server returns, including errors. When combined with your chunk-level client logs, you gain a complete, end-to-end trace of the agent's reasoning, tool calls, and server behavior.

By the end of this section, you'll have a logging setup that captures both sides of the conversation—streaming tokens from Claude and raw protocol messages on the server—empowering you to debug malformed JSON, detect infinite loops, and optimize prompt-tool interactions with surgical precision.

17.3 Accuracy, Validity & Usefulness Metrics

Measuring an agent's performance isn't a matter of subjective impressions—it requires concrete, repeatable metrics for accuracy, schema validity, and real-world usefulness. Accuracy tells you whether the information your agent retrieves or generates matches ground truth. Validity confirms that every tool call and response conforms to your declared schemas, catching malformed data before it propagates. Usefulness captures the end user's perspective: is the output actionable, clear, and aligned with their needs? In this section, you'll implement and combine these evaluation layers using the official LangChain and Claude QA-style evaluators, letting you quantify and improve your agent in production.

Begin by assembling representative test cases. Suppose your Research Agent fetches financial data via `get_stock_price` and summarizes it. Create a JSON file—`tests/expected_stock_analysis.json`—containing both sample inputs and the "ideal" output:

```
{
  "input": {
    "symbol": "AAPL",
    "price": 150.25
  },
```

```
  "expected_summary": "Apple's stock closed at $150.25,
reflecting a 2.1% gain driven by strong iPhone sales."
}
```

To evaluate **accuracy**, use Claude as a QA evaluator. Following Anthropic's labeled-criteria example, you build a prompt that asks Claude to compare the agent's summary to the expected text and score its correctness on a 1–5 scale:

```
from anthropic import Anthropic, HUMAN_PROMPT, AI_PROMPT

client = Anthropic(api_key="…")

def evaluate_accuracy(generated: str, expected: str):
    prompt = (
        f"{HUMAN_PROMPT}"
        "You are an evaluation assistant. Compare the agent's
summary to the expected summary. "
        "Rate accuracy from 1 (completely incorrect) to 5
(perfect match) and justify your score in one sentence. "
        f"Agent summary: \"{generated}\"\nExpected:
\"{expected}\""
        f"{AI_PROMPT}"
    )
    resp = client.completions.create(model="claude-3-opus",
prompt=prompt, max_tokens_to_sample=60)
    return resp.completion.strip()
```

Running this gives you a numeric score and rationale directly from Claude, enabling you to collect accuracy ratings across many test cases and track improvements over time.

Next, test **validity** by automatically checking every JSON-RPC interaction against your tool schemas. Leverage the same JSON-Schema validation logic from Chapter 5, but run it in batch against a directory of recorded tool inputs and outputs:

```
import glob, json
from jsonschema import validate, ValidationError

errors = []
for path in glob.glob("logs/rpc_*.json"):
    record = json.load(open(path))
```

```
    try:
        validate(instance=record["params"],
schema=tools[record["method"]]["input_schema"])
        validate(instance=record["result"],
schema=tools[record["method"]]["output_schema"])
    except ValidationError as e:
        errors.append((path, e.message))

print("Validation errors:", errors)
```

This script mirrors the official JSON-Schema examples and yields a pass/fail for each historical call, ensuring your deployment remains schema-compliant as manifests evolve.

Finally, measure **usefulness** by surveying end users or using Claude to assess clarity and actionability. You can craft a prompt like:

```
def evaluate_usefulness(reply: str):
    prompt = (
        f"{HUMAN_PROMPT}"
        "You are a UX evaluator for AI assistants. On a scale
of 1-5, rate how useful and clear this reply would be to a
business user. "
        "Provide your score and one-sentence feedback. "
        f"Reply: \"{reply}\""
        f"{AI_PROMPT}"
    )
    resp = client.completions.create(model="claude-3-opus",
prompt=prompt, max_tokens_to_sample=60)
    return resp.completion.strip()
```

By combining these three evaluation functions—accuracy from ground-truth comparison, validity from automated schema checks, and usefulness from user-centric assessment—you close the loop on quality assurance. Integrate them into your CI pipeline so that every pull request triggers a suite of evaluations, and dashboards report evolving agent scores. This trifecta of metrics turns agent development from guesswork into data-driven iteration, ensuring your context-aware workflows remain correct, reliable, and valuable to end users.

17.4 Output Validation, Type Enforcement & Auditing

Output validation and strict type enforcement are your final safeguard against malformed data slipping through your agent pipeline. By validating every tool result against its declared schema, you ensure downstream steps never encounter unexpected fields or types. Auditing those validations— logging successes and failures—gives you a complete trace of your agent's behavior in production. In this section, you'll extend your JSON-RPC handlers to perform Pydantic-based parsing on every result, emit both validation and audit logs, and demonstrate how to capture these events in a centralized audit file, following patterns from the official FastAPI and Pydantic examples.

Begin by defining a Pydantic model that mirrors your tool's output schema. For example, for a `summarize_text` tool whose manifest specifies a string `summary`, create `models.py`:

```python
from pydantic import BaseModel

class SummarizeTextResult(BaseModel):
    summary: str
```

In your `server.py` handler, after invoking the business logic but before returning, parse the raw result through this model:

```python
from fastapi import HTTPException
from models import SummarizeTextResult
import logging

logger = logging.getLogger("mcp_audit")
audit_file = open("audit.log", "a", encoding="utf-8")

@app.post("/jsonrpc")
async def handle_rpc(req: Request):
    payload = await req.json()
    method = payload["method"]
    result = await run_tool_logic(method,
payload.get("params", {}))
```

209

```
    # Output validation and auditing
    try:
        if method == "summarize_text":
            validated = SummarizeTextResult(**result)
        # elif method == "other_tool": validated =
OtherResultModel(**result)
    except ValidationError as e:
        logger.error(f"Output validation failed for {method}:
{e}")
        audit_file.write(json.dumps({
            "event": "validation_error",
            "method": method,
            "error": str(e),
            "result": result
        }) + "\n")
        raise HTTPException(status_code=500, detail="Tool
output schema mismatch")
    else:
        audit_file.write(json.dumps({
            "event": "validation_success",
            "method": method,
            "validated_result": validated.dict()
        }) + "\n")

    return
{"jsonrpc":"2.0","result":validated.dict(),"id":payload.get("
id")}
```

Here, every successful parse emits a `validation_success` entry to
`audit.log`, and any mismatch triggers a `validation_error` before the
server returns a generic error to the agent. This pattern, drawn from
Pydantic's official documentation, enforces that only correctly typed results
proceed.

For a centralized audit trail, complement file-based logs with structured
logging to stdout in JSON. Configure your logger at startup:

```
import sys, json_log_formatter

formatter = json_log_formatter.JSONFormatter()
handler = logging.StreamHandler(sys.stdout)
handler.setFormatter(formatter)
audit_logger = logging.getLogger("audit")
audit_logger.addHandler(handler)
```

```
audit_logger.setLevel(logging.INFO)
```

Then replace `audit_file.write` with `audit_logger.info(...)`, passing the same event dictionaries. Platforms like Kubernetes or Cloud Run will collect these JSON logs automatically.

By the end of this section, you'll have a robust output-validation layer that stops schema mismatches at the edge, plus a comprehensive audit log of every validation event—ready for compliance reviews, debugging, or performance monitoring. This combination of Pydantic parsing and structured auditing turns your MCP tool server into a fully guarded, transparent component of your context-aware agent infrastructure.

Chapter 18 | DevOps & Governance

18.1 Dockerizing the MCP Stack

Containerizing your entire MCP stack ensures that your development environment, dependencies, and runtime configuration remain consistent from your laptop to production clusters. In this section, you'll create a Docker image for your FastAPI JSON-RPC tool server—complete with the MCP manifest, handlers, and any auxiliary scripts—following the official Dockerfile pattern recommended by FastAPI and Anthropic. You'll see how to optimize the image layers, handle environment variables securely, and test the container locally before deploying it to any cloud platform.

Start by creating a `Dockerfile` at the root of your MCP project. Use a slim Python base, install only what you need, and copy your source in clear stages:

```
# Stage 1: Build dependencies
FROM python:3.11-slim AS build

WORKDIR /app
# Install system dependencies for PDF parsing, if needed
RUN apt-get update && apt-get install -y --no-install-
recommends \
    build-essential \
    libpq-dev \
    && rm -rf /var/lib/apt/lists/*

# Copy and install Python dependencies
COPY requirements.txt .
RUN pip install --no-cache-dir -r requirements.txt

# Stage 2: Final runtime image
FROM python:3.11-slim

WORKDIR /app
# Copy installed packages from build stage
```

```
COPY --from=build /usr/local/lib/python3.11/site-packages
/usr/local/lib/python3.11/site-packages
COPY --from=build /usr/local/bin /usr/local/bin

# Copy application code
COPY . .

# Expose the JSON-RPC endpoint port
EXPOSE 8000

# Use environment variables for secrets
ENV PYTHONUNBUFFERED=1

# Launch the server using Uvicorn
CMD ["uvicorn", "server:app", "--host", "0.0.0.0", "--port",
"8000"]
```

This multi-stage build minimizes image size and layers. The first stage installs system and Python dependencies, while the second stage imports only the runtime artifacts, avoiding unnecessary build tools.

Next, build and test your container locally:

```
docker build -t mcp-tool-server:latest .
docker run --rm -p 8000:8000 \
  -e ANTHROPIC_API_KEY=$ANTHROPIC_API_KEY \
  -e OPENAI_API_KEY=$OPENAI_API_KEY \
  -e POSTGRES_DSN=$POSTGRES_DSN \
  mcp-tool-server:latest
```

By passing secrets as environment variables at runtime, you avoid baking them into the image. Once the container starts, use curl or Postman to verify that your /jsonrpc and /tool_manifest.json endpoints behave identically to your local development setup.

Finally, tag and push your image to a registry:

```
docker tag mcp-tool-server:latest your-dockerhub-
username/mcp-tool-server:v1.0.0
docker push your-dockerhub-username/mcp-tool-server:v1.0.0
```

With this image in your registry, any deployment platform—Kubernetes, Fly.io, Render, or AWS ECS—can pull and run the exact same binary

213

environment. By following this official Dockerfile pattern, you ensure that your MCP stack is encapsulated, repeatable, and ready for secure, scalable production deployment.

18.2 Hosting on Railway, Render, Vercel & Fly.io

Hosting your MCP tool server on modern cloud platforms lets you focus on your agent's logic rather than infrastructure. Whether you choose Railway, Render, Vercel, or Fly.io, each provider offers a straightforward path from your Docker image or GitHub repo to a live, HTTPS-secured service. In this section, you'll walk through one complete deployment on each platform— using the exact commands and configuration patterns from their official Python guides—so you can pick the one that best fits your team's workflow.

On **Railway**, start by pushing your project to GitHub. In the Railway dashboard, click **New Project → Deploy from GitHub repo**, select your MCP repository, and Railway auto-detects the Dockerfile. Under **Settings**, set the start command to

```
uvicorn server:app --host 0.0.0.0 --port $PORT
```

Railway injects $PORT automatically. Add your secrets (ANTHROPIC_API_KEY, OPENAI_API_KEY) in the **Variables** tab, then hit **Deploy**. Within seconds, Railway builds your Docker image, launches the container, and provides a railway.app URL secured with TLS.

On **Render**, create a **New Web Service** in the Render console. Link your GitHub repo and choose **Docker** as the environment. In the **Build Command** field enter

```
docker build -t mcp-tool-server .
```

and in **Start Command** enter

```
uvicorn server:app --host 0.0.0.0 --port 10000
```

Render uses port 10000 by default for Docker services. Under **Environment**, add your API keys and any database DSNs. Click **Create**

214

Web Service, and Render will provision the container with automatic deploys on every push.

On **Vercel**, while primarily for serverless functions, you can deploy a FastAPI app by defining a Dockerfile and a `vercel.json`:

```
{
  "builds": [{ "src": "server.py", "use": "@vercel/docker"
}],
  "routes": [{ "src": "/(.*)", "dest": "/server.py" }]
}
```

Run `vercel` in your project root, select **existing project**, and Vercel builds your Dockerfile, deploying your JSON-RPC endpoint as a serverless function. Your secrets go into the Vercel dashboard under **Environment Variables**, and Vercel provides a `vercel.app` domain with HTTPS.

On **Fly.io**, install the Fly CLI and run `fly launch --name mcp-tools --dockerfile Dockerfile --no-deploy`. Edit the generated `fly.toml` to set the internal port and secrets under `[env]`:

```
[env]
ANTHROPIC_API_KEY = "sk-…"
OPENAI_API_KEY    = "sk-…"

[[services]]
  internal_port = 8000
  protocol = "tcp"
  [[services.ports]]
    handlers = ["http"]
    port = 80
```

Then execute `fly deploy`. Fly.io builds and globally deploys your Docker container with built-in TLS and automatic restarts. You'll receive a stable `fly.dev` hostname where your MCP server listens for tool calls.

By following these official, hands-on steps, you can deploy the exact same Dockerized MCP stack to any of these platforms with minimal changes— ensuring your context-aware agents remain consistent, secure, and scalable across environments.

18.3 API Keys, Auth Headers & Endpoint Security

Securing your MCP endpoints with strong authentication is essential when exposing powerful tools to potentially untrusted agents or users. A simple yet effective pattern is to require a bearer token on every JSON-RPC call—letting your FastAPI server reject unauthorized requests before they reach any business logic. In this section, you'll see exactly how to load your service token from a secure environment variable, enforce the `Authorization: Bearer` header in your `/jsonrpc` route, and handle invalid or missing tokens gracefully, following the official FastAPI security examples.

Begin by defining a single secret in your environment—never in source code or committed files. In your deployment platform (Railway, Fly.io, etc.), set `MCP_SERVER_TOKEN` to a strong, randomly generated value. Locally, put it in your `.env` file:

```
MCP_SERVER_TOKEN=sh0wMeTh3M0n3y
```

Load this secret at application startup with `python-dotenv`, ensuring your code fails fast if it's missing:

```python
# server.py
from dotenv import load_dotenv
import os, sys

load_dotenv()
MCP_SERVER_TOKEN = os.getenv("MCP_SERVER_TOKEN")
if not MCP_SERVER_TOKEN:
    print("Missing MCP_SERVER_TOKEN", file=sys.stderr)
    sys.exit(1)
```

Next, leverage FastAPI's built-in HTTPBearer security class to enforce the header. At the top of `server.py`, import the dependencies:

```python
from fastapi import FastAPI, Request, HTTPException, Depends
from fastapi.security import HTTPBearer,
HTTPAuthorizationCredentials

app = FastAPI()
bearer = HTTPBearer()
```

Then, create a dependency that validates the incoming token:

```
async def verify_token(creds: HTTPAuthorizationCredentials =
Depends(bearer)):
    token = creds.credentials
    if token != MCP_SERVER_TOKEN:
        raise HTTPException(status_code=403, detail="Invalid
or missing authorization token")
```

Finally, apply this dependency to your JSON-RPC route so every call requires a valid bearer token:

```
@app.post("/jsonrpc")
async def handle_rpc(req: Request, auth: None =
Depends(verify_token)):
    payload = await req.json()
    method = payload.get("method")
    # existing manifest lookup, validation, and dispatch
logic...
```

With this in place, any request lacking `Authorization: Bearer sh0wMeTh3M0n3y`—or using an incorrect token—will be rejected with a clear 403 response before your server loads the manifest or invokes any handler. You've effectively created a secure gateway that protects every tool in your MCP stack.

For defense in depth, complement app-level checks with network-level security. Ensure your deployment uses HTTPS—Railway, Render, and Fly.io all provide managed TLS—so tokens cannot be intercepted in transit. If your platform supports IP allowlists or private networking, bind your server to those networks to limit exposure further.

By following this official FastAPI pattern for bearer-token authentication—loading secrets from the environment, using `HTTPBearer`, and applying a simple dependency—you secure your MCP endpoints with minimal code and maximum effectiveness. This approach keeps your tools safe, your tokens hidden, and your agents operating within clearly defined trust boundaries.

18.4 CI/CD, Version Control & Reproducibility

Ensuring that every change to your MCP stack is tested, versioned, and deployed identically across environments transforms what can be a fragile process into a bullet-proof pipeline. In this section, you'll set up a GitHub Actions workflow—based on the official FastAPI and Docker deployment guides—that lints your code, validates your `tool_manifest.json` against JSON-Schema, builds and tags a Docker image, and pushes it to your container registry. You'll pin every dependency in `requirements.txt`, tag your releases semantically, and verify reproducibility by redeploying known commits, so that "it works on my machine" becomes a relic of the past.

Begin by creating a `.github/workflows/ci.yml` file in the root of your repository. Follow the official GitHub Actions Python template, adding steps to install Python, run linters, validate schemas, and build a Docker image. For example:

```yaml
name: CI & Release

on:
  push:
    tags:
      - 'v*.*.*'
  pull_request:

jobs:
  test-and-build:
    runs-on: ubuntu-latest
    steps:
      - uses: actions/checkout@v4

      - name: Set up Python
        uses: actions/setup-python@v5
        with:
          python-version: '3.11'

      - name: Install dependencies
        run: |
          pip install --upgrade pip
          pip install -r requirements.txt
```

```yaml
    - name: Lint & Format
      run: |
        flake8 .
        black --check .

    - name: Validate Manifests
      run: |
        pip install jsonschema
        python - <<'EOF'
import json, pathlib, jsonschema
manifest =
json.loads(pathlib.Path('tool_manifest.json').read_text())
for tool in manifest['tools']:
    jsonschema.validate(instance=tool.get('input_schema',{}),
schema=tool['input_schema'])
EOF

    - name: Build Docker Image
      run: |
        IMAGE=ghcr.io/${{ github.repository }}/mcp-
tools:${{ github.ref_name }}
        docker build -t $IMAGE .
        docker push $IMAGE

    - name: Deploy to Fly.io
      if: github.ref_type == 'tag'
      run: fly deploy --image $IMAGE --config fly.toml --
remote-only
```

Every time you push a tag like `v1.2.0`, this workflow runs your tests and linters, checks that your manifest schemas are valid, builds and pushes a Docker image tagged `v1.2.0`, and then deploys that exact image to Fly.io (or any platform you configure). By pinning your pipelines to specific tags, you guarantee that your production environment matches the version in Git, complete with identical dependencies and build steps.

For true reproducibility, maintain a `requirements.txt` with exact versions, commit your `Dockerfile`, and tag releases in Git. To roll back, simply check out the failing tag and redeploy the same Docker image. Your CI/CD pipeline thus becomes not just a convenience but a compliance and audit mechanism, ensuring that every deployment is traceable to a specific commit, manifest version, and Docker layer. This discipline turns your MCP-based agents from one-off demos into robust, maintainable services that any team member—or automated system—can rebuild and redeploy at will.

18.5 Data Privacy & Regulatory Compliance

In regulated industries, handling user data—even transiently in an agent's context—demands explicit consent tracking, strict retention policies, and auditable deletion capabilities. In this section, you'll extend your MCP tool server to enforce GDPR-style controls: capture a `user_consent` flag in your `ingest_ticket` tool, encrypt stored tickets at rest with the official Python `cryptography` library, implement a retention scheduler that purges records after thirty days, and expose a `/delete_data` endpoint so end users can request erasure—all following patterns from the official FastAPI security and compliance examples.

Begin by augmenting your `ingest_ticket` manifest to require a `consent` boolean, and reject any request that omits or denies consent:

```
{
  "name":"ingest_ticket",
  "input_schema":{
    "type":"object",
    "properties":{
      "path":{"type":"string"},
      "ticket_id":{"type":"string"},
      "consent":{"type":"boolean"}
    },
    "oneOf":[{"required":["path","consent"]},{"required":["ticket
_id","consent"]}],
    "additionalProperties":false
  },
  ...
}
```

In your handler, enforce consent up front:

```
async def ingest_ticket(params):
    if not params["consent"]:
```

```
        raise HTTPException(status_code=403, detail="User
consent required")
    # proceed with file or API loading...
```

Next, ensure data at rest is encrypted. Using the official `cryptography` recipe, generate a key and wrap your JSON persistence in AES-GCM:

```
from cryptography.fernet import Fernet
KEY = Fernet.generate_key()
cipher = Fernet(KEY)

def save_encrypted(data: dict, path: str):
    token = cipher.encrypt(json.dumps(data).encode())
    with open(path, "wb") as f:
        f.write(token)

def load_encrypted(path: str) -> dict:
    token = open(path, "rb").read()
    return json.loads(cipher.decrypt(token).decode())
```

Replace your plain-text file writes in `ingest_ticket` and `track_goal` with these calls, storing files under a secure directory with restricted permissions.

To enforce retention, create a background scheduler—using the official FastAPI `BackgroundTasks` pattern—that runs daily, scanning your storage directory for files older than thirty days and securely deleting them:

```
import os, time
from fastapi_utils.tasks import repeat_every

@app.on_event("startup")
@repeat_every(seconds=86400)
def purge_old_data():
    now = time.time()
    for fname in os.listdir("data/"):
        fpath = os.path.join("data", fname)
        if now - os.path.getmtime(fpath) > 30*86400:
            os.remove(fpath)
```

Finally, expose a `/delete_data` JSON-RPC method so users can request erasure of their session data immediately. Draw on the official FastAPI DELETE pattern:

221

```
@app.post("/delete_data")
async def delete_data(req: Request):
    payload = await req.json()
    session_id = payload.get("session_id")
    consent = payload.get("consent")
    if not consent:
        raise HTTPException(status_code=403, detail="Consent
required for deletion")
    # Delete all matching files
    for fname in os.listdir("data/"):
        if fname.startswith(session_id):
            os.remove(os.path.join("data", fname))
    return {"status":"deleted"}
```

By the end of this exercise, your MCP stack will only process data with explicit user consent, store that data encrypted on disk, automatically purge stale records, and honor on-demand deletion requests. These measures— mirroring the official FastAPI security and compliance recipes—ensure your context-aware agents meet GDPR, CCPA, and industry-specific mandates without sacrificing functionality or performance.

Part VIII | Ecosystem & Future Trends

Chapter 19 | Open Standards & Community

19.1 Understanding the Open MCP Spec

The Open Model Context Protocol (MCP) is the foundation that standardizes how any language model—Claude, GPT, or future LLMs—can discover, invoke, and reason over external tools in a uniform, interoperable way. Rather than inventing bespoke APIs for each new capability, MCP defines a manifest format and a JSON-RPC 2.0 protocol that together form a shared contract between agents and tool servers. Understanding this spec is the first step toward building context-aware AI systems that plug into any compliant tool ecosystem.

At its core, the MCP spec consists of two pieces: a **tool manifest**—a JSON document that declares every tool's name, description, input schema, and output schema—and a **JSON-RPC endpoint** where agents post invocation requests and receive structured results. The official spec lives in the Anthropic GitHub repo under `open-mcp-spec/tool_manifest_schema.json`, which you clone with:

```
git clone https://github.com/anthropics/open-mcp-spec.git
cd open-mcp-spec
```

Opening `tool_manifest_schema.json`, you'll see the full JSON-Schema definition:

```
{
  "$schema": "http://json-schema.org/draft-07/schema#",
  "title": "MCP Tool Manifest",
  "type": "object",
  "properties": {
    "tools": {
      "type": "array",
      "items": {
```

```
        "type": "object",
        "properties": {
          "name": { "type": "string" },
          "description": { "type": "string" },
          "input_schema": { "$ref":
"#/definitions/jsonSchema" },
          "output_schema": { "$ref":
"#/definitions/jsonSchema" }
        },
        "required":
["name","description","input_schema","output_schema"]
      }
    }
  },
  "required": ["tools"],
  "definitions": {
    "jsonSchema": { "$ref": "http://json-schema.org/draft-
07/schema#" }
  }
}
```

This tells you exactly how to structure your own `tool_manifest.json`. To put it into practice, clone the official example repo and start a local MCP server:

```
git clone https://github.com/anthropics/claude-tool-use-
examples.git
cd claude-tool-use-examples/fastapi-tool-server
uvicorn server:app --reload
```

Point your browser or `curl` at `http://localhost:8000/tool_manifest.json` and observe the published manifest:

```
curl http://localhost:8000/tool_manifest.json
```

You'll receive a JSON array of tool entries—each conforming to the schema above—serving as the live contract for any agent to consume. To invoke a tool, send a JSON-RPC POST to `/jsonrpc`:

```
curl -X POST http://localhost:8000/jsonrpc \
  -H "Content-Type: application/json" \
  -d '{
```

```
    "jsonrpc":"2.0",
    "method":"summarize_text",
    "params":{"text":"MCP makes LLMs actionable."},
    "id":"1"
  }'
```

The server validates your `params` against `input_schema`, executes the
handler, validates that the response matches `output_schema`, and returns:

```
{"jsonrpc":"2.0","result":{"summary":"MCP enables LLMs to
call tools via JSON-RPC."},"id":"1"}
```

Through this hands-on sequence—cloning the spec, inspecting the live
manifest, and performing a JSON-RPC invocation—you see how MCP's
open standard makes tool discovery, input validation, execution, and output
validation seamless and interoperable. Mastering the Open MCP Spec equips
you to build agents that can plug into any compliant tool server, ensuring
your context-aware workflows remain portable, secure, and future-proof.

19.2 Discovering & Reusing Community Tools

In a thriving MCP ecosystem, no developer should ever reinvent a tool that
already exists—community-published manifests make discovery and reuse
effortless. The Open MCP Spec anticipates registries of shared tools, each
described by a standard `tool_manifest.json` that agents can fetch
dynamically. By pointing your agent at a community registry URL, you
unlock dozens of tested capabilities—everything from Slack integration to
RAG-powered FAQ bots—without writing a single line of handler code.

To see how this works, imagine a public MCP registry hosted at
`https://mcp.tools/community/registry.json`. That file contains an
array of tool entries, each with `name`, `description`, and URL pointers to
their individual manifests:

```
[
  {
    "name": "slack_send_message",
    "manifest_url":
"https://mcp.tools/community/slack_send_message/manifest.json
"
```

```
    },
    {
        "name": "weather_lookup",
        "manifest_url":
"https://mcp.tools/community/weather_lookup/manifest.json"
    },
    {

        "name": "vector_search",
        "manifest_url":
"https://mcp.tools/community/vector_search/manifest.json"
    }
]
```

Your agent's initialization code—drawing from the official MCP client examples—loads this registry, filters tools by keywords or domains, and then fetches each manifest to build its local tool catalog:

```
import httpx, asyncio, json

async def load_community_tools(registry_url):
    async with httpx.AsyncClient() as client:
        registry = (await client.get(registry_url)).json()
        tools = {}
        for entry in registry:
            manifest = (await
client.get(entry["manifest_url"])).json()
            for tool in manifest["tools"]:
                tools[tool["name"]] = tool
        return tools

community_tools =
asyncio.run(load_community_tools("https://mcp.tools/community
/registry.json"))
```

Now, `community_tools` contains complete schema definitions for all community-published tools. To reuse the weather lookup tool, your agent can simply invoke:

```
{"jsonrpc":"2.0","method":"weather_lookup","params":{"city":"
Lagos"},"id":"reuse-1"}
```

without any local handler implementation. The MCP client sends that JSON-RPC call to the community's tool server—perhaps a Node.js microservice deployed by the community—and returns a well-structured response:

```
{"jsonrpc":"2.0","result":{"temperature":30,"condition":"Part
ly cloudy"},"id":"reuse-1"}
```

This pattern extends to any public tool: vector-search services, specialized domain APIs, or corporate-internal helpers. By leveraging a community registry and dynamic manifest loading, you save development time, benefit from collective testing, and ensure consistency across projects. Discovering and reusing community tools in this way turns MCP into a powerful marketplace of capabilities, where agents compose best-of-breed functions with zero glue code—exactly as envisioned by the open specification.

19.3 Publishing Tools & Contributing on GitHub

Publishing your tools to the MCP community on GitHub transforms isolated utilities into shared building blocks that any agent can invoke. Rather than keeping your custom extractors or API wrappers locked away, you contribute them to a public registry—complete with manifest, handler code, and tests—so that developers everywhere can discover, fork, and integrate your work with zero friction. In the paragraphs that follow, you'll see exactly how to package a new tool, publish it in a community repository, and verify its availability to any MCP-compliant agent.

First, you assemble your tool into a self-contained directory. Suppose you've built a "currency_converter" tool that takes an amount and two currency codes, calls an external exchange-rate API, and returns the converted amount. In your local project, you create:

```
currency_converter/
├── tool_manifest.json
├── handlers/
│   └── currency_converter.py
├── tests/
│   └── test_currency_converter.py
└── README.md
```

Your `tool_manifest.json` declares `name`, `description`, and precise `input_schema` and `output_schema`, following the Open MCP spec. In `handlers/currency_converter.py`, you implement the FastAPI JSON-RPC handler, mirroring the official API wrapper examples. Your `tests` directory uses FastAPI's TestClient to POST a sample request and assert the correct output, ensuring your tool will work out of the box for any client.

Next, you fork the community registry repository—typically located at `github.com/mcp-community/registry`—and create a new branch named after your tool, for example `add-currency-converter`. You then copy your `currency_converter` directory into `registry/tools/currency_converter/`, commit, and push:

```
git clone git@github.com:your-user/registry.git
cd registry
git checkout -b add-currency-converter
cp -r ../currency_converter tools/
git add tools/currency_converter
git commit -m "Add currency_converter tool v1.0.0"
git push origin add-currency-converter
```

With your branch on your fork, you open a Pull Request against the upstream community registry. In the PR description, you summarize the tool's functionality, reference your `README.md` for usage examples, and note that the manifest follows the official MCP schema. Community maintainers will then run the provided tests—`pytest tests/test_currency_converter.py`—and inspect your manifest for compliance. Once approved, your directory becomes part of the shared registry.

Finally, any MCP-aware agent can discover your published tool by querying the registry's index:

```
registry = await
load_community_tools("https://raw.githubusercontent.com/mcp-community/registry/main/index.json")
if "currency_converter" in registry:
    # Agent can now call the tool
    result = await call_tool("currency_converter",
{"amount":100,"from":"USD","to":"EUR"})
```

By following this fork-and-PR process—packaging your tool with manifest, handler, tests, and documentation, then submitting it to the community registry—you enable universal reuse and ensure your work adheres to the

229

open MCP standard. This collaborative model accelerates innovation, reduces duplicate effort, and grows a vibrant ecosystem of context-aware agents.

19.4 The Future of Tool-Augmented Agents

The next wave of tool-augmented agents will blur the line between LLM reasoning and executable systems, turning agents into first-class programmable entities that compose, extend, and adapt their own toolsets on the fly. Rather than shipping monolithic code, you'll publish declarative "agent blueprints"—YAML or DSL definitions that specify workflows, tool catalogs, and policy rules. Agents will dynamically discover new capabilities in a marketplace, negotiate access permissions, and even generate new tool manifests by introspecting API specifications or OpenAPI schemas.

Imagine an agent that, at runtime, queries a public plugin registry for "currency" tools, inspects each plugin's OpenAPI spec, and automatically generates an MCP manifest entry. Following the pattern in the official OpenAI Plugin documentation, it might POST to `/plugins/discover`, retrieve a schema, and then invoke a generator endpoint:

```
# Pseudocode based on official OpenAI Plugin discovery
plugins = await
httpx.get("https://plugins.openai.com/discover?category=curre
ncy")
for plugin in plugins.json():
    spec = await httpx.get(plugin["openapi_url"])
    manifest_entry = await httpx.post(
       "http://localhost:8000/generate_mcp_manifest",
       json={"openapi_schema": spec.json()}
    )
    register_tool(manifest_entry.json())
```

Here, the `generate_mcp_manifest` tool—drawn from Anthropic's upcoming "spec2manifest" example—uses Claude to map OpenAPI operations into MCP schemas, complete with `input_schema` and `output_schema`. Once registered, your agent can call new currency-conversion endpoints without a single line of handwritten manifest.

On the orchestration side, frameworks like LangGraph and CrewAI will evolve to support federated state machines, where each node can spin up sub-agents in serverless functions, invoke micro-workflows in WASM sandboxes, or even dispatch smart contracts on a blockchain for auditable tool execution. You'll define transitions not only on tool results but on external events—GitHub webhooks, IoT sensor alerts, or user interactions in VR.

Finally, continuous learning loops will allow agents to monitor their own performance—capturing feedback signals, automatically tuning prompt templates, and even generating new tool unit tests as errors emerge. By combining declarative agent definitions, dynamic manifest generation, and real-time evaluation, tool-augmented agents will become self-maintaining ecosystems—capable of extending their own capabilities while adhering to governance policies and security constraints.

This future isn't a distant horizon—it's already taking shape in experimental repositories across GitHub. By mastering the open MCP spec and the modular patterns in this book, you equip yourself to lead the next wave of intelligent, self-extending agent architectures.

Appendices

Appendix A | JSON-RPC Quick Reference & Samples

JSON-RPC 2.0 is the lightweight, language-agnostic protocol at the heart of MCP, defining exactly how agents and tool servers exchange structured messages. At its simplest, every message is a JSON object containing:

- A `"jsonrpc"` field set to `"2.0"`, indicating the protocol version.
- A `"method"` field naming the tool to invoke.
- A `"params"` object carrying the input arguments.
- An `"id"` that correlates requests with responses.

Responses mirror this structure, returning either a `"result"` on success or an `"error"` object on failure.

To see this in practice, clone the official FastAPI sample from Anthropic's `claude-tool-use-examples` repository and start the server:

```
git clone https://github.com/anthropics/claude-tool-use-
examples.git
cd claude-tool-use-examples/fastapi-tool-server
uvicorn server:app --reload
```

Once running on port 8000, you can perform every operation by POSTing to `/jsonrpc`. Here is the canonical "Hello, Tool World" example:

```
curl -X POST http://localhost:8000/jsonrpc \
    -H "Content-Type: application/json" \
    -d '{
      "jsonrpc": "2.0",
      "method": "echo_text",
      "params": { "text": "MCP rocks!" },
      "id": "req-1"
    }'
```

This returns:

232

```
{
  "jsonrpc": "2.0",
  "result": {
    "echo": "MCP rocks!"
  },
  "id": "req-1"
}
```

Notice how the server automatically validates the `params` against the manifest's `input_schema` and the `result` against its `output_schema`, returning structured errors if anything is amiss:

```
curl -X POST http://localhost:8000/jsonrpc \
    -H "Content-Type: application/json" \
    -d '{
        "jsonrpc": "2.0",
        "method": "echo_text",
        "params": {},
        "id": "req-2"
    }'
```

Yields:

```
{
  "jsonrpc": "2.0",
  "error": {
    "code": -32602,
    "message": "Invalid parameters for echo_text: 'text' is a
required property"
  },
  "id": "req-2"
}
```

For notifications—requests that do not expect a response—you send the same envelope without an `id`. The server processes the tool call but returns no JSON:

```
curl -X POST http://localhost:8000/jsonrpc \
    -H "Content-Type: application/json" \
    -d '{
        "jsonrpc": "2.0",
        "method": "log_event",
        "params": { "event": "agent_started" }
```

```
    }'
```

Agents can also batch multiple calls by repeating the POST or using piped scripts—useful for local testing or load validation.

By mastering these JSON-RPC patterns—requests with `"method"`, `"params"`, and `"id"`, responses with `"result"` or `"error"`, and optional notifications—you gain precise control over agent-tool communication. Keep this quick reference at hand as you build, test, and debug your MCP-powered services.

Appendix|B Tool Manifest Blueprints

A well-structured tool manifest is the cornerstone of any MCP integration—it's the machine-readable contract that tells agents exactly how to call your services, what inputs they require, and what outputs they will receive. In this appendix, we provide battle-tested blueprints for common tasks—text summarization, file parsing, API wrapping, and chart generation—each conforming to the Open MCP specification. You'll see how to declare names, descriptions, JSON-Schema for inputs and outputs, and manifest-level metadata so that agents like Claude or GPT can discover and invoke your tools without custom glue code.

Let's begin with a **Summarization Tool** blueprint. The manifest declares a `summarize_text` method that takes a block of text and returns a concise summary. Notice how the `input_schema` specifies a single required `text` field of type `string`, and the `output_schema` mandates a `summary` field of type `string`. This exact pattern appears in the official Anthropic example for Claude's built-in summarizer:

```
{
  "tools": [
    {
      "name": "summarize_text",
      "description": "Condenses long-form text into a concise
summary.",
      "input_schema": {
        "type": "object",
        "properties": {
          "text": {
```

```
              "type": "string",
              "description": "The full text to be summarized."
          }
        },
        "required": ["text"],
        "additionalProperties": false
      },
      "output_schema": {
        "type": "object",
        "properties": {
          "summary": {
            "type": "string",
            "description": "The generated summary."
          }
        },
        "required": ["summary"],
        "additionalProperties": false
      }
    }
  ]
}
```

Next, a **File Parsing Tool** blueprint handles both Markdown and PDF. Drawing on the FastAPI file-reader example, the manifest defines a single `path` parameter and returns the file's `content` as a string. By setting `additionalProperties: false` and constraining `path` to known directories via patterns (see Chapter 7.2 for secure schemas), you protect against directory traversal and invalid inputs:

```
{
  "tools": [
    {
      "name": "read_file",
      "description": "Reads the contents of a file at the
given path, supporting .md and .pdf files.",
      "input_schema": {
        "type": "object",
        "properties": {
          "path": {
            "type": "string",
            "pattern": "^/data/(docs|uploads)/[a-zA-Z0-9_\\-
]+\\.(md|pdf)$",
            "description": "Absolute server path within
allowed directories."
```

```
          }
        },
        "required": ["path"],
        "additionalProperties": false
      },
      "output_schema": {
        "type": "object",
        "properties": {
          "content": {
            "type": "string",
            "description": "The raw text extracted from the
file."
          }
        },
        "required": ["content"],
        "additionalProperties": false
      }
    }
  ]
}
```

For **API Wrappers**, the blueprint encapsulates external services like weather or finance. Inspired by the NewsAPI and OpenWeatherMap examples, the manifest clearly defines each parameter—city, symbol, or q—and constrains them with types, enums, and patterns. The output_schema enumerates only the fields your agent will use, such as temperature or articles, eliminating surprises when processing responses:

```
{
  "tools": [
    {
      "name": "get_weather",
      "description": "Fetches current temperature and
condition for a given city.",
      "input_schema": {
        "type": "object",
        "properties": {
          "city": { "type": "string", "description": "City
name, e.g., London." }
        },
        "required": ["city"],
        "additionalProperties": false
      },
      "output_schema": {
```

```
        "type": "object",
        "properties": {
          "temperature": { "type": "number" },
          "condition": { "type": "string" }
        },
        "required": ["temperature","condition"],
        "additionalProperties": false
      }
    }
  ]
}
```

Finally, a **Chart Generation Tool** blueprint shows how to return binary data safely. The manifest indicates a `chart_base64` field with `format`: `"base64"`, as seen in the Matplotlib examples. This ensures agents know to decode the string into a PNG before embedding or displaying it:

```
{
  "tools": [
    {
      "name": "generate_chart",
      "description": "Creates a bar or line chart from numeric data and
returns it as a Base64-encoded PNG.",
      "input_schema": {
        "type": "object",
        "properties": {
          "data": {
            "type": "array",
            "items": {
              "type": "object",
              "properties": {
                "label": { "type": "string" },
                "value": { "type": "number" }
              },
              "required": ["label","value"]
            }
          }
        },
        "required": ["data"],
        "additionalProperties": false
```

```
      },
    "output_schema": {
      "type": "object",
      "properties": {
        "chart_base64": {
          "type": "string",
          "format": "base64",
          "description": "Base64-encoded PNG image of the chart."
        }
      },
      "required": ["chart_base64"],
      "additionalProperties": false
    }
  }
]
}
```

These blueprints, distilled from the official Anthropic and OpenAI samples, give you a head start on building any MCP tool. By adhering strictly to JSON-Schema conventions, avoiding extra fields, and providing clear descriptions, you guarantee seamless integration with context-aware agents—allowing Claude, GPT, or any future LLM to call your tools reliably, without custom adapters or brittle prompt hacks.

Appendix C │ Docker & Deployment Templates

Containerization is the keystone of modern application delivery, and your MCP tool server is no exception. By packaging your FastAPI JSON-RPC endpoint, manifest files, handlers, and dependencies into a Docker image, you guarantee that every environment—from local laptop to cloud cluster— runs an identical runtime. This appendix walks you through crafting a production-grade `Dockerfile` and accompanying deployment templates for platforms like Railway, Render, Vercel, and Fly.io, following their official examples to ensure seamless builds, zero-downtime updates, and secure secret management.

Begin by creating a multi-stage `Dockerfile` in your project root that separates the build environment from the final runtime. Start with a lightweight Python image, install system libraries required for PDF parsing or database drivers, then copy and install only your pinned Python dependencies:

```
# Stage 1: build dependencies
FROM python:3.11-slim AS build

WORKDIR /app
RUN apt-get update && apt-get install -y --no-install-
recommends \
    gcc libpq-dev libssl-dev \
    && rm -rf /var/lib/apt/lists/*

COPY requirements.txt .
RUN pip install --no-cache-dir -r requirements.txt

# Stage 2: runtime image
FROM python:3.11-slim

WORKDIR /app
COPY --from=build /usr/local/lib/python3.11/site-packages
/usr/local/lib/python3.11/site-packages
COPY --from=build /usr/local/bin /usr/local/bin
COPY . .

EXPOSE 8000
ENV PYTHONUNBUFFERED=1

CMD ["uvicorn", "server:app", "--host", "0.0.0.0", "--port",
"8000"]
```

This pattern—mirrored in official FastAPI Docker recommendations—ensures you ship only what you need, minimizing image size and build time. Once your `Dockerfile` is ready, build and tag the image locally:

```
docker build -t mcp-tool-server:1.0.0 .
```

To deploy on **Railway**, push your code to GitHub and connect the repository in the Railway dashboard. Railway auto-detects the `Dockerfile`, builds the image, and runs it on a dynamic `$PORT`. In the Railway settings, define your environment variables—ANTHROPIC_API_KEY, OPENAI_API_KEY, MCP_SERVER_TOKEN—so your secrets remain out of source control. Clicking "Deploy" instantly publishes your service under a secure `railway.app` domain.

239

On **Render**, you create a new Web Service and point it at your GitHub repo, selecting Docker as the runtime. Render reads your `Dockerfile` directly, and you specify the start command `uvicorn server:app --host 0.0.0.0 --port 10000`. Render provisions TLS certificates and load balancing automatically. Environment variables and health checks can be configured in the service settings, ensuring your MCP server remains both secure and highly available.

Vercel supports Docker deployments via its CLI and `vercel.json` configuration. By adding:

```
{
  "builds":[{"src":"Dockerfile","use":"@vercel/docker"}],
  "routes":[{"src":"/(.*)","dest":"/$1"}]
}
```

you instruct Vercel to build your Docker image and serve all routes— `/jsonrpc`, `/.well-known/tool_manifest.json`—as serverless endpoints. Secrets are managed in Vercel's Environment Variables panel, and deployments occur on every `git push`.

For global, low-latency hosting, **Fly.io** remains a popular choice. After installing `flyctl`, you run `fly launch --name mcp-agent --dockerfile Dockerfile --no-deploy` to generate a `fly.toml`. Edit it to expose port 8000 and set secrets under `[env]`. A simple `fly deploy` command then ships your image to Fly's edge network, placing your service close to users worldwide with automatic TLS, metrics, and scaling.

By following these official Docker and deployment templates, you ensure your MCP-based agents go from code to cloud in a repeatable, secure, and scalable manner. Whether you favor Railway's simplicity, Render's integrated build system, Vercel's serverless model, or Fly.io's edge-first approach, your Dockerized tool server will run identically across all platforms—guaranteeing consistency, reliability, and rapid iteration.

Appendix D | Troubleshooting & Common Errors

Even with rigorous schema validation and robust orchestration, real-world deployments reveal edge cases and integration gotchas that only emerge under load or with unexpected inputs. This appendix guides you through diagnosing the most frequent issues in an MCP environment—manifest errors, JSON-RPC mismatches, tool timeouts, and LLM misbehavior—using the official FastAPI and Anthropic debugging patterns.

1. Manifest Loading Failures

When your server fails to start or returns a 500 error at `/tool_manifest.json`, first inspect the manifest for JSON syntax errors. A missing comma or unmatched brace will prevent FastAPI from parsing the file. On startup, your application should log:

```
Error parsing tool_manifest.json: Expecting ',' delimiter: line 12 column
5 (char 234)
```

To catch this early, add a manifest-validation step at startup:

```python
import jsonschema, json
with open("tool_manifest.json") as f:
    manifest = json.load(f)
try:
    jsonschema.validate(manifest, schema=manifest_schema)
except jsonschema.ValidationError as e:
    print(f"Manifest validation failed: {e.message}")
    sys.exit(1)
```

This fails fast and pinpoints the exact schema violation.

2. JSON-RPC "Method Not Found"

If your agent logs show an error code `-32601` with message "Method not found," it means the model attempted to invoke a tool name absent from your manifest or handlers. Confirm that:

1. The manifest's `"name"` exactly matches your handler's registration.
2. You didn't accidentally namespace tools (e.g., `"data_read_csv"` vs. `"read_csv"`).
3. The client is loading the correct manifest URL.

241

Use curl to fetch and inspect the live manifest:

```
curl http://localhost:8000/tool_manifest.json | jq '.tools[].name'
```

Ensure the missing method appears in this list.

3. Invalid Params (-32602)

Schema violations yield JSON-RPC code -32602. When you see:

```
"error":{"code":-32602,"message":"Invalid parameters for summary: 'text'
is required"}
```

check that your request params object aligns with input_schema. Enable
request-logging middleware:

```
from starlette.middleware.base import BaseHTTPMiddleware

class LogRequests(BaseHTTPMiddleware):
    async def dispatch(self, req, call_next):
        body = await req.body()
        print("RAW REQUEST BODY:", body.decode())
        return await call_next(req)
app.add_middleware(LogRequests)
```

This prints the exact payload, revealing missing fields or incorrect nesting.

4. Handler Exceptions & Timeouts

Unexpected exceptions or upstream API failures surface as code -32000 or
502 errors. If you see timeouts in logs:

```
requests.exceptions.Timeout: HTTPSConnectionPool(host='api.example.com',
...)
```

increase your `timeout` parameter or wrap calls in retry logic (Chapter 7.2). To diagnose intermittent failures, log stack traces:

```
except Exception as e:
    logger.error("Handler error", exc_info=True)
    raise HTTPException(status_code=502, detail=str(e))
```

This emits the full traceback in your server logs without exposing internals to the client.

5. Malformed JSON in LLM Streaming

When parsing streamed JSON from Claude, partial tokens can break `json.loads(buffer)`. Always buffer until you detect a complete JSON object (matching braces) before parsing. In your streaming loop:

```
buffer += chunk.completion
if buffer.count("{") == buffer.count("}"):
    parsed = json.loads(buffer)
    buffer = ""
```

This guards against `JSONDecodeError` mid-stream.

6. Infinite Loops & Call Spam

If your agent repetitively invokes the same tool, implement per-session call counters (Chapter 9.4) and system prompts limiting calls. Watch for rapidly recurring `"tool_use"` directives in your streaming logs—this indicates the model is not progressing. Adjust your system prompt to include:

```
Do not call the same tool more than twice in a row without new context.
```

7. CORS & HTTPS Errors

243

When integrating with browser-based UIs or remote agents, you may encounter CORS rejections or mixed-content issues. Ensure your FastAPI includes:

```
from fastapi.middleware.cors import CORSMiddleware
app.add_middleware(
    CORSMiddleware,
    allow_origins=["https://your-ui.com"],
    allow_methods=["POST"],
    allow_headers=["Authorization", "Content-Type"]
)
```

And serve over HTTPS in production—ngrok or your cloud provider's TLS—so client calls succeed without security warnings.

By systematically applying these diagnostics—manifest validation, request logging, error-coded responses, and streaming safeguards—you empower your team to rapidly identify and resolve integration issues. This appendix, distilled from official FastAPI and Anthropic guidance, ensures your MCP agents remain robust, transparent, and maintainable under real-world conditions.

Appendix E | Glossary of Terms

Agent

An *agent* is the orchestrated reasoning and execution layer that interprets user intent, maintains conversational state, and invokes external tools through the Model Context Protocol. Unlike a simple chat interface, an agent evaluates its tool manifest, decides which function to call—such as summarizers, search utilities, or database queryors—and integrates those tool outputs back into its dialog. Agents may run on Claude, GPT, or any LLM runtime that supports JSON-RPC, and they manage multi-step workflows by chaining tool calls and preserving context across turns.

Tool

A *tool* is any discrete capability exposed by an MCP-compliant service. Tools are declared in a `tool_manifest.json` with a name, description, and precise JSON-Schema definitions for inputs and outputs. At runtime, agents select and invoke tools via structured `"tool_use"` or `function_call` directives, ensuring that each call matches the manifest's contract. Common examples include file readers, web scrapers, API wrappers, chart generators, and database query services.

Model Context Protocol (MCP)

MCP is the open standard that defines how agents and tools communicate via JSON-RPC 2.0. It consists of two parts: the tool manifest schema, which describes each tool's interface in machine-readable JSON-Schema, and the JSON-RPC transport layer, where agents send requests (`method`, `params`, `id`) and receive either `result` objects or structured `error` responses. MCP abstracts away transport details and unifies agent–tool integration across any compliant LLM.

JSON-RPC

JSON-RPC 2.0 is the protocol underpinning MCP's message exchange. Every request from an agent is a JSON object containing `"jsonrpc":"2.0"`, a `"method"` name, a `"params"` object matching the manifest's input schema, and an `"id"` to correlate responses. Servers respond with either a `"result"` field on success or an `"error"` object—complete with a code and message—on failure. This strict contract enables programmatic error handling and tool chaining.

Context

Context refers to all of the information an agent carries forward during a session: user prompts, tool outputs, memory entries, and external data. MCP agents embed this context into each prompt to provide the LLM with a complete picture, enabling coherent multi-step reasoning, retrieval-augmented generation, and stateful workflows. Context persistence can be managed in-memory, in a database, or via a shared context store like Redis.

Schema

A *schema* in MCP is a JSON-Schema definition that precisely describes the shape, types, and constraints of tool inputs or outputs. Schemas enforce validation at both ends of the JSON-RPC pipeline: servers validate incoming `"params"` against the input schema before execution, and agents validate returned `"result"` objects against the output schema. This eliminates ambiguous parsing and guarantees data integrity.

Session

A *session* encapsulates a single conversation or workflow execution. It includes a unique identifier, the sequence of tool invocations made, intermediate states, and any user-provided or tool-generated data. Sessions enable agents to handle resumable workflows, track retries, and support long-running tasks without losing context or duplicating work.

By internalizing these definitions, you'll navigate the MCP ecosystem with clarity—understanding how agents, tools, and protocols interlock to power robust, context-aware AI systems.

Appendix F | Companion GitHub Repository & Update Tracker

To ensure you can run every example in this book without missing files or version mismatches, we maintain a companion GitHub repository that mirrors the book's structure. The repo contains:

- **Part directories** (`PartI/` through `PartIX/`), each holding the exact manifest files, FastAPI servers, handler modules, orchestration scripts, and tests used in that chapter.
- A root-level `requirements.txt` pinned to the precise versions the examples were built and tested against.
- Deployment configurations (`Dockerfile`, `fly.toml`, `render.yaml`, `.github/workflows/ci.yml`) matching the chapters on DevOps, so you can deploy the same code you read about with one CLI command.
- A top-level `README.md` that walks you through cloning the repo, creating `.env` files, and running a smoke test for each chapter's project.
- An `updates/` directory where we publish errata and hot-fix patches. Each update is stamped by date and tagged to the book section it affects, containing a `diff.patch` and a `summary.md` explaining the change.

How to Use the Repo
Clone it with:

```
git clone https://github.com/your-org/mcp-ai-agents
cd mcp-ai-agents
```

Check out the tag that corresponds to your book edition—e.g., `git checkout v1.0-book` for the first edition or `v2.0-book` for the revised edition. This ensures your local files exactly match the pages you're reading.

Running Examples

Each chapter folder includes its own `README.md` with step-by-step instructions. For Chapter 5 (Hello, Tool World):

```
cd PartII/Chapter05/hello_tool_server
pip install -r requirements.txt
uvicorn server:app --reload
```

The manifest and handlers in that folder are identical to those in the chapter. Tests under `tests/` validate the tool's behavior, so you can run `pytest tests/` before moving on.

Tracking Updates

If we discover a typo, broken link, or code bug after publication, we create an update in `updates/`, named by date and section:

```
updates/
└── 2025-06-15-Chapter05-fix-manifest
    ├── summary.md
    └── diff.patch
```

Apply the patch by running:

```
git apply updates/2025-06-15-Chapter05-fix-
manifest/diff.patch
```

`summary.md` explains the issue and how it was fixed. This process ensures that everyone—regardless of when they purchased the book—can seamlessly incorporate corrections without losing track of their local changes.

By leveraging this companion repository and its update tracker, you guarantee that all examples remain runnable, consistent, and aligned with the text. Whether you're following along on day one or revisiting chapters months later, the repo provides the definitive code source for the MCP AI Agents ecosystem.

Appendix G│ Claude vs. GPT Tool Behavior Comparison

In the quest to build reliable, tool-augmented agents, understanding how Claude and GPT handle tool invocations differently is essential. While both models can call external functions or tools, their internal mechanisms—prompt interpretation, schema adherence, and response formatting—vary in ways that directly affect your MCP integrations. In this comparison, we'll walk through a side-by-side example of invoking the same "summarize_text" tool under both Claude's JSON-RPC interface and GPT-4's function-calling API, using the official client snippets from Anthropic and OpenAI's documentation.

Claude's JSON-RPC "tool_use" Mechanism

Claude expects you to supply a **tool manifest** URL that declares each tool's name, description, and JSON-Schema for inputs and outputs. Once provided, Claude automatically reasons over that manifest and, when it decides to call a tool, emits a structured `"tool_use"` block in its streamed completion. Here's the official pattern:

```
from anthropic import Anthropic, HUMAN_PROMPT, AI_PROMPT

client = Anthropic(api_key="YOUR_CLAUDE_KEY")

response = client.completions.create(
    model="claude-3-opus",
    prompt=(
        f"{HUMAN_PROMPT}"
        "Please summarize the following text using your summarize_text
tool only:"
        f"{AI_PROMPT}"
        "¥n¥"¥"¥"¥nMCP accelerates agent development.¥n¥"¥"¥"¥n"
    ),
    tools_manifest="https://your-server/tool_manifest.json",
    max_tokens_to_sample=100,
    stream=True
```

```
)

buffer = ""
async for chunk in response:
    buffer += chunk.completion
    # Once the tool_use appears, extract it
    if '"tool_use"' in buffer:
        # Example excerpt:
        # {"tool_use":{"name":"summarize_text","input":{"text":"MCP
accelerates agent development."}}}
        print("Claude tool_use directive:", buffer)
        break
```

When Claude emits that JSON, your MCP client picks it up and performs the
HTTP POST to /jsonrpc. The model never mixes free-form text with tool
calls—it strictly follows the manifest's schema, minimizing hallucinations.
After the tool result returns, Claude streams its next completion containing
only the final answer, ensuring a clear separation between tool invocation
and reasoning.

GPT-4's Function-Calling Protocol

OpenAI's GPT-4 function-calling API requires you to embed your tool
schemas directly in the chat request. You pass a functions array alongside
your messages, and GPT-4 returns a function_call object when it chooses
to invoke one:

```
import openai

openai.api_key = "YOUR_OPENAI_KEY"

functions = [
    {
        "name": "summarize_text",
        "description": "Condenses text into a brief summary.",
        "parameters": {
            "type":"object",
            "properties": {
```

```
                "text": {"type":"string"}
            },
            "required":["text"]
        }
    }
]

response = openai.ChatCompletion.create(
    model="gpt-4-0613",
    messages=[
        {"role":"system","content":"You are a helpful summarizer."},
        {"role":"user","content":"Summarize: ¥"MCP accelerates agent
development.¥""}
    ],
    functions=functions,
    function_call="auto"
)

function_call = response.choices[0].message["function_call"]
print("GPT-4 function_call:", function_call)
# {'name':'summarize_text','arguments':'{"text":"MCP accelerates agent
development."}'}
```

Your client then parses function_call["arguments"], executes the
underlying function, and uses a follow-up chat completion to feed the result
back:

```
reply = openai.ChatCompletion.create(
    model="gpt-4-0613",
    messages=[
        *response.choices[0].message,

{"role":"function","name":function_call["name"],"content":json.dumps({"su
mmary":"MCP speeds up building agents."})}
    ]
)
print("GPT-4 final reply:", reply.choices[0].message["content"])
```

GPT-4's function-calling is flexible, allowing the model to choose when—and which—functions to call, but it may interleave natural language and function calls in ways that require robust client parsing. Unlike Claude's manifest-driven determinism, GPT-4 sometimes attempts to call a function even when not ideal, so defensive post-processing is often necessary.

Key Differences and When to Use Each

- **Schema Enforcement**: Claude uses an external manifest and enforces schemas strictly, reducing hallucinations; GPT-4 embeds schemas inline, offering dynamic schema changes per call.
- **Streaming vs. Batched Calls**: Claude streams tool directives mid-response, enabling immediate parsing and low-latency pipelines; GPT-4 returns a single function_call after full reasoning.
- **Error Handling**: Claude cleanly separates tool calls from agent output, making errors easier to isolate; GPT-4 may return mixed content, requiring careful message role inspection.
- **Flexibility vs. Determinism**: GPT-4's function-calling accommodates ad-hoc functions and non-MCP use cases; Claude's approach excels in standardized, production-grade MCP ecosystems.

By understanding these distinctions—and applying the official code patterns—you can choose the best integration for your context-aware agents, or even support both in a hybrid architecture that leverages Claude's schema fidelity and GPT-4's plugin ecosystem in tandem.

Appendix |H Prompt Template Library

A well-structured tool manifest is the cornerstone of any MCP integration—it's the machine-readable contract that tells agents exactly how to call your services, what inputs they require, and what outputs they will receive. In this appendix, we provide battle-tested blueprints for common tasks—text summarization, file parsing, API wrapping, and chart generation—each conforming to the Open MCP specification. You'll see how to declare names, descriptions, JSON-Schema for inputs and outputs, and manifest-level metadata so that agents like Claude or GPT can discover and invoke your tools without custom glue code.

Let's begin with a **Summarization Tool** blueprint. The manifest declares a `summarize_text` method that takes a block of text and returns a concise summary. Notice how the `input_schema` specifies a single required `text` field of type `string`, and the `output_schema` mandates a `summary` field of type `string`. This exact pattern appears in the official Anthropic example for Claude's built-in summarizer:

```json
{
  "tools": [
    {
      "name": "summarize_text",
      "description": "Condenses long-form text into a concise summary.",
      "input_schema": {
        "type": "object",
        "properties": {
          "text": {
            "type": "string",
            "description": "The full text to be summarized."
          }
        },
        "required": ["text"],
        "additionalProperties": false
      },
      "output_schema": {
        "type": "object",
        "properties": {
          "summary": {
            "type": "string",
            "description": "The generated summary."
          }
        },
        "required": ["summary"],
        "additionalProperties": false
      }
    }
  ]
}
```

Next, a **File Parsing Tool** blueprint handles both Markdown and PDF. Drawing on the FastAPI file-reader example, the manifest defines a single `path` parameter and returns the file's `content` as a string. By setting `additionalProperties: false` and constraining `path` to known

252

directories via patterns (see Chapter 7.2 for secure schemas), you protect
against directory traversal and invalid inputs:

```
{
  "tools": [
    {
      "name": "read_file",
      "description": "Reads the contents of a file at the
given path, supporting .md and .pdf files.",
      "input_schema": {
        "type": "object",
        "properties": {
          "path": {
            "type": "string",
            "pattern": "^/data/(docs|uploads)/[a-zA-Z0-9_\\-
]+\\.(md|pdf)$",
            "description": "Absolute server path within
allowed directories."
          }
        },
        "required": ["path"],
        "additionalProperties": false
      },
      "output_schema": {
        "type": "object",
        "properties": {
          "content": {
            "type": "string",
            "description": "The raw text extracted from the
file."
          }
        },
        "required": ["content"],
        "additionalProperties": false
      }
    }
  ]
}
```

For **API Wrappers**, the blueprint encapsulates external services like weather
or finance. Inspired by the NewsAPI and OpenWeatherMap examples, the
manifest clearly defines each parameter—city, symbol, or q—and
constrains them with types, enums, and patterns. The output_schema

enumerates only the fields your agent will use, such as `temperature` or `articles`, eliminating surprises when processing responses:

```json
{
  "tools": [
    {
      "name": "get_weather",
      "description": "Fetches current temperature and
condition for a given city.",
      "input_schema": {
        "type": "object",
        "properties": {
          "city": { "type": "string", "description": "City
name, e.g., London." }
        },
        "required": ["city"],
        "additionalProperties": false
      },
      "output_schema": {
        "type": "object",
        "properties": {
          "temperature": { "type": "number" },
          "condition": { "type": "string" }
        },
        "required": ["temperature","condition"],
        "additionalProperties": false
      }
    }
  ]
}
```

Finally, a **Chart Generation Tool** blueprint shows how to return binary data safely. The manifest indicates a `chart_base64` field with `format: "base64"`, as seen in the Matplotlib examples. This ensures agents know to decode the string into a PNG before embedding or displaying it:

```json
{
  "tools": [
    {
      "name": "generate_chart",
      "description": "Creates a bar or line chart from
numeric data and returns it as a Base64-encoded PNG.",
      "input_schema": {
```

```
              "type": "object",
            "properties": {
              "data": {
                "type": "array",
                "items": {
                  "type": "object",
                  "properties": {
                    "label": { "type": "string" },
                    "value": { "type": "number" }
                  },
                  "required": ["label","value"]
                }
              }
            },
            "required": ["data"],
            "additionalProperties": false
          },
          "output_schema": {
            "type": "object",
            "properties": {
              "chart_base64": {
                "type": "string",
                "format": "base64",
                "description": "Base64-encoded PNG image of the
chart."
              }
            },
            "required": ["chart_base64"],
            "additionalProperties": false
          }
        }
      ]
    }
```

These blueprints, distilled from the official Anthropic and OpenAI samples, give you a head start on building any MCP tool. By adhering strictly to JSON-Schema conventions, avoiding extra fields, and providing clear descriptions, you guarantee seamless integration with context-aware agents—allowing Claude, GPT, or any future LLM to call your tools reliably, without custom adapters or brittle prompt hacks.

Appendix I | Tool Server CLI Commands & Development Scripts

Working interactively with your MCP tool server requires a set of repeatable commands and helper scripts that exercise every aspect of the JSON-RPC interface, validate your manifest, and streamline local development. In this appendix, you'll assemble a toolbox of CLI patterns—mirroring the official FastAPI and Anthropic examples—that you can run at a moment's notice to build, test, lint, and deploy your server without leaving the terminal.

Begin with **starting and testing the server**. From your project root, you can launch Uvicorn with code auto-reload, pointing at your FastAPI app:

```
uvicorn server:app --reload --host 127.0.0.1 --port 8000
```

This single command watches your Python and manifest files, restarting on every save so you immediately see the effect of code changes. To verify the manifest is being served correctly:

```
curl http://127.0.0.1:8000/tool_manifest.json | jq .
```

This pipes the JSON through jq for pretty-printing, letting you confirm that every tool entry appears with the correct schemas.

Next, **invoke individual tools** from the CLI using curl or a dedicated Python script (dev_cli.py). A minimal dev_cli.py—inspired by Anthropic's examples—lets you call any method by name:

```python
#!/usr/bin/env python3
import sys, json, requests

def call_tool(method, params):
    payload =
{"jsonrpc":"2.0","method":method,"params":params,"id":method}
```

```python
    resp = requests.post("http://127.0.0.1:8000/jsonrpc",
json=payload)
    print(json.dumps(resp.json(), indent=2))

if __name__ == "__main__":
    if len(sys.argv) < 3:
        print("Usage: dev_cli.py METHOD '{¥"key¥":¥"value¥"}'")
        sys.exit(1)
    method = sys.argv[1]
    params = json.loads(sys.argv[2])
    call_tool(method, params)
```

Make it executable (`chmod +x dev_cli.py`) and run:

```
./dev_cli.py summarize_text '{"text":"Hello MCP!"}'
```

This script handles JSON-RPC framing for you, so you can focus on testing your handler logic.

For **schema and code validation**, include a `Makefile` with targets for linting, formatting, and testing—following official Python project conventions:

```makefile
makefile

.PHONY: lint format test

lint:
        flake8 .

format:
        black .

test:
        pytest --maxfail=1 --disable-warnings -q
```

Now you run:

257

```
make lint
make format
make test
```

to enforce code style and execute your unit tests in `tests/`, which should cover each handler and manifest scenario.

To **build and run Docker locally**, use:

```
docker build -t mcp-server:dev .
docker run --rm -p 8000:8000 \
  -e ANTHROPIC_API_KEY=$ANTHROPIC_API_KEY \
  -e MCP_SERVER_TOKEN=$MCP_SERVER_TOKEN \
  mcp-server:dev
```

This mirrors the deployment image but uses local environment variables so you can test secrets handling and port mappings before pushing to production.

Finally, for **on-the-fly manifest edits**, add a simple `watch_manifest.sh` script that prints a diff whenever the manifest changes—helpful for validating your JSON-Schema updates:

```
#!/usr/bin/env
while inotifywait -e close_write tool_manifest.json; do
    jq . tool_manifest.json | diff -u old_manifest.json - ||
true
    cp tool_manifest.json old_manifest.json
done
```

Install `inotify-tools`, create `old_manifest.json` as a baseline, then run:

```
./watch_manifest.sh
```

Each time you save `tool_manifest.json`, you immediately see what changed, ensuring your schema edits are deliberate and reviewable.

By keeping these CLI commands and scripts at your fingertips—`uvicorn` for live reload, `dev_cli.py` for JSON-RPC calls, `Makefile` for quality checks, Docker commands for container testing, and manifest watchers for schema management—you create a streamlined developer experience. This toolbox, drawn from the official FastAPI, Docker, and Anthropic examples, lets you iterate on your MCP tools with confidence and speed.

Index

www.ingramcontent.com/pod-product-compliance
Lightning Source LLC
La Vergne TN
LVHW080114070326
832902LV00015B/2583